180 Days of HIGH-FREQUENCY WORDS for Prekindergarten

Darcy Mellinger, M.A.T., NBCT

Publishing Credits

Corinne Burton, M.A.Ed., *Publisher*
Emily R. Smith, M.A.Ed., *SVP of Content Development*
Véronique Bos, *Vice President of Creative*
Lynette Ordoñez, *Content Manager*
Carol Huey-Gatewood, M.A.Ed., *Editor*
David Slayton, *Assistant Editor*
Jill Malcolm, *Graphic Designer*

Standards

© Copyright 2010 National Governors Association Center for Best Practices and Council of Chief State School Officers. All rights reserved.
© Copyright 2007–2022 Texas Education Agency (TEA). All Rights Reserved.
© 2012 English–Language Arts Content Standards for California Public Schools by the California Department of Education.
© 2022 TESOL International Association
© 2022 Board of Regents of the University of Wisconsin System

Image Credits: pp. 26, 48, 95, 110, 142, 174 Jill Malcolm; all other images from iStock and/or Shutterstock

A division of Teacher Created Materials
5482 Argosy Avenue
Huntington Beach, CA 92649
www.tcmpub.com/shell-education
ISBN 978-1-0876-6265-7
© 2023 Shell Educational Publishing, Inc.
Printed in China
51497

Table of Contents

What Do the Experts Say?

Welcome to *180 Days of High-Frequency Words for Prekindergarten*! In this book, students will learn key words to help prepare them for the challenges of reading. These practice pages can also be useful for older students who need extra support in learning high-frequency words.

Foundations

Practicing foundational skills will give young readers a great advantage as they prepare for reading. Repetition is a key to success for new readers. It is estimated that 85–90 percent of brain growth occurs in the first five years of life (First Things First 2017). In this book, students practice high-frequency words, which are the words that occur most frequently in written and spoken sentences. The acquisition of high-frequency words is a foundation for other reading skills, such as fluency, vocabulary, and comprehension.

These words do not necessarily follow the rules of phonics and should be read with automaticity to save time and mental attention for other reading tasks. They are often critical connectors within phrases and sentences (Fry and Kress 2006).

Including high-frequency words in early literacy instruction promotes automaticity with commonly encountered words. Automaticity builds fluency in independent reading and leads to higher comprehension. When children recognize high-frequency words by sight, they avoid expending mental energy to decode these words using phonics strategies. They are able to focus more on fluency and comprehension.

A term that is often used interchangeably for high-frequency words is *sight words*. The idea behind calling high-frequency words *sight words* is that children will know a word upon sight. This is achieved using several teaching strategies that are embedded in *180 Days of High-Frequency Words for Prekindergarten*. In the *Journal of the Virginia State Reading Association*, Heather P. Warley et al. describe strategies for facilitating high-frequency and sight word learning in this way:

> Sight words do not become sight words by rote visual memorization techniques such as flash cards. They become sight words through multiple opportunities to read, write, and analyze words both in and out of context. When children are provided the skills needed to read, as well as the time to practice applying those skills, they will start to remember words they have seen before in context. They will create a strong mental "entry" of a word that allows them to automatically retrieve all of the word's information at once, including its pronunciation and meaning. Literacy instruction that is focused around the child's developmental stage and that provides varied opportunities to interact with words will facilitate students' sight word learning (Warley, Invernizzi, and Drake 2015, 44).

A child's knowledge of the high-frequency words in this book will prepare them for reading success for years to come. Learning to recognize these 50 high-frequency words with automaticity is a key component for that success.

What Do the Experts Say? *(cont.)*

Repetition

A key to mastering high-frequency words is repetition, repetition, repetition! The 50 words practiced in this book were selected from the beginning lists of words in Edward Fry's *1,000 Instant Words: The Most Common Words for Teaching Reading, Writing, and Spelling* (1999).

The 50 words are organized with two days to connect with each word upon introduction. Then, after learning 10 words, students will review them to increase repetition. Children engage with the words in many different, interactive ways. Additionally, throughout the book, students will enjoy cumulative reviews of all the high-frequency words they have previously learned. This repetition will help students refresh their memories of these words with the ultimate goal of the words becoming long-term memories.

Practice Pages

The activities in this book reinforce prekindergarten reading skills in a variety of ways. Each full page of practice is easy to prepare. You may use these pages to start the morning routine, launch the day's reading lesson, or provide follow-up lessons. Regardless of how the pages are used, students will be engaged in practicing the foundational skills to learn how to read and build a sight-word vocabulary of frequently encountered words through these standards-based activities.

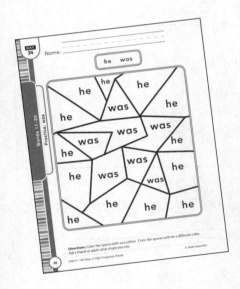

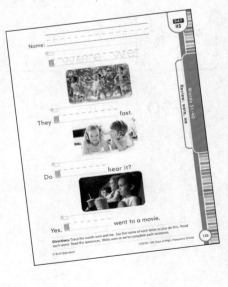

What Do the Experts Say? *(cont.)*

Fry Instant Word List

Edward Fry (1925–2010) was a professor, researcher, and prolific author on topics related to learning to read. His research led him to publish lists of the most frequently used words in the English language—the *New Instant Word List* in 1957 and an updated version in 1980. Fry asserted that beginning readers should master a basic sight vocabulary of common words and a high-frequency vocabulary. Today, his *Instant Word List* of 1,000 high-frequency words is used extensively by teachers for literacy instruction.

In this book, students will learn the first 50 words (shown below) and engage in activities to read them with automaticity upon sight. When students read high-frequency and simple words, they feel like detectives cracking a code. The more high-frequency words students know, the more successful they will be when reading sentences in text.

Fry Instant Word List—Words 1–50

1–10	the	of	and	a	to	in	is	you	that	it
11–20	he	was	for	on	are	as	with	his	they	I
21–30	at	be	this	have	from	or	one	had	by	words
31–40	but	not	what	all	were	we	when	your	can	said
41–50	there	use	an	each	which	she	do	how	their	if

How to Use This Book

Using the Practice Pages

The practice pages in this book provide instructional opportunities for each of the 180 days of the school year. Activities are organized by the introduction, practice, and review of five groups of 10 words from Dr. Fry's list. Teachers may plan to prepare packets of the practice pages for students. Each day's activities are aligned to the reading standards that can be found on page 12.

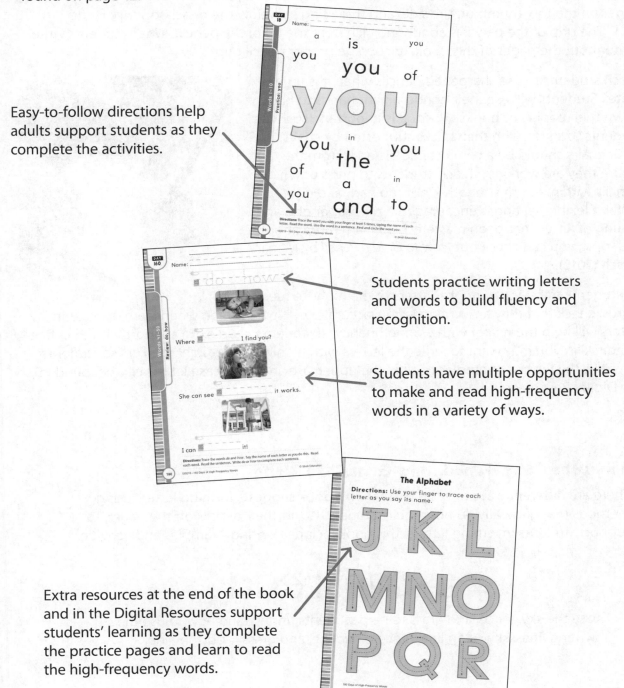

Easy-to-follow directions help adults support students as they complete the activities.

Students practice writing letters and words to build fluency and recognition.

Students have multiple opportunities to make and read high-frequency words in a variety of ways.

Extra resources at the end of the book and in the Digital Resources support students' learning as they complete the practice pages and learn to read the high-frequency words.

How to Use This Book (cont.)

Letter Formation and Proper Pencil Grip

It is important for children to learn how to properly grip their pencils early. Students will naturally find their dominant hands. If a student writes with both their right and their left hand, brain research indicates that it is preferred to allow them to write with both hands. Younger students may have to grow into their grip, so encourage students to try this grip when you see that they are ready. The best pencil grip for children is with their pointer finger on the top, thumb on the side, and three fingers below the pencil to support the grip. The grip of the pencil is about one inch from the tip of the pencil. When students write throughout the pages of this book, encourage proper pencil grip.

Teach students to use sharpened pencils when it is time to write. Students will use their nondominant hands to hold down their papers or books. Posture is important, so invite students to sit tall with their backs supported by chairs. Their chairs should be a comfortable distance from the table where they are working. Teach students to press down on pencils with medium strength—not too hard and not too softly. Flexible seating is encouraged after proper grip and writing of letters has been mastered. To learn more about this topic, you can check out *How to Hold a Pencil* by Megan Hirsch (2010).

As students trace and write the letters of the high-frequency words, check that they are writing letters accurately. The repetition when learning to write letters will help them later with writing fluency. If students need extra support with their fine-motor skills, you may want to write the letters with highlighters or light markers so students can trace the letters. Examples of all of the uppercase and lowercase letters can be found in the Digital Resources.

Using the "Sky, Fence, and Grass" to Write

There are different ways to write letters. This book suggests forming letters using methods that generally do not require students to lift their pencils off the page. To support students in writing letters, this book includes writing examples and activities.

Use the sky, fence, and grass to help students understand how to use the writing lines: sky = top line, fence = midline, and grass = bottom line.

Activities Overview

In this book, students will explore the following activities on their early literacy journey.

Activity	Description
Color by High-Frequency Word	Children color each section of an image based on the high-frequency words and a color code key.
Draw About Words	After completing color by high-frequency words activities, children draw and color pictures to extend their learning.
Finish Phrases	Learners write high-frequency words to finish phrases.
Fun with Phrases	Students read phrases, use pictures to infer meaning, and write the missing high-frequency words in the phrases.
Hide the Words	Students read the words, draw pictures, and hide words in pictures.
Hunt for Words	Students trace, color, and read a high-frequency word. They use it in a sentence, and then they circle the word within the pages of a book.
Looking at Letters	Children trace the shapes of the letters and words to become familiar with each word.
Matching Game	Students play a matching game to review high-frequency words.
Matching Words	Learners draw lines to match high-frequency words in two columns.
Scavenger Hunt	Children go on scavenger hunts to find the words in print in their own environments.
Shape of Words	Students use the shapes of high-frequency words to write the letters in the correct boxes and read the completed stories.
Story in Order	Children read sentences with high-frequency words and put stories in the correct order.
Story Time	Students finish each story by writing the correct high-frequency words.
Trace the Word	Students trace high-frequency words in sentences, using the pictures to help derive meaning.
Word Search	Children hunt in the word search to find the day's high-frequency word.
Word Splash	Children look at a page filled with review words to find one word.
Words in Text	Students find the high-frequency word within the text on the page of a provided book.

Activities Overview *(cont.)*

Review Activities

Activity	Description
Coin Flip for Words	Children flip coins to determine which high-frequency words to read on a gameboard.
Color Words	Students color circles that form the letters of high-frequency words.
Crayon Art	Children use crayons and watercolors to reveal words.
Hidden Words	Students find words hidden in pictures.
Hopscotch with Words	Learners review high-frequency words while playing hopscotch.
Tapping Words	Children play a game to see how many high-frequency words they are able to tap in 1 minute.
Vowels in Words	Students use a key to color high-frequency words based on the vowels in each review word.
Word Jar Shake Game*	Children shake high-frequency words out of their Word Jars to read the words that land faceup.
Words in Light	Learners use a flashlight to trace high-frequency words.
Words in Print	Children see how many high-frequency words they can find in print.

*Have students each create a Word Jar by decorating a plain glass or plastic jar with a lid. Have students store their cut-out *High-Frequency Word Cards* in their jars. Encourage students to review these words on the review days.

Activities Overview *(cont.)*

Assessment and Diagnosis

Determine Baseline

When assessing in early childhood classrooms, educators must consider children's developmental levels in all learning domains. To assess mastery of high-frequency words, first determine a baseline of knowledge by checking for understanding. Determining the baseline serves as a beginning point of instruction. The recording sheets on pages 204–205 can be used to document students' baseline mastery of the 50 high-frequency words and to record increasing mastery during formal checkpoints throughout the year. The *High-Frequency Word Cards* for words 1–10, 11–20, 21–30, 31–40, and 41–50 can be viewed during assessment.

Progress Monitoring

Formal or diagnostic assessments should be conducted periodically—usually once a semester or at the beginning, middle, and end of the school year. These formal assessments can be used to determine if a child is thriving under the current curriculum or if changes are necessary to meet the child's needs. Educators may determine how many word lists to assess during each term. The *Class Recording Sheet* on page 205 can be used to document class mastery on the high-frequency word lists, as well as to record words that individual students have not yet mastered.

On the last day of practice (Day 180), you may use the certificate on page 203 to celebrate students' learning achievements.

Standards Correlations

Shell Education is committed to producing educational materials that are research and standards based. To support this effort, this resource is correlated to the academic standards of all 50 states, the District of Columbia, the Department of Defense Dependent Schools, and the Canadian provinces. A correlation is also provided for key professional educational organizations.

To print a customized correlation report for your state, please visit our website at **www.tcmpub.com/administrators/correlations** and follow the online directions. If you require assistance in printing correlation reports, please contact the Customer Service Department at 1-800-858-7339.

College and Career Readiness Standards

The activities in this book are aligned to the following college and career readiness (CCR) standards:

Print Concepts	• Recognize and name all upper- and lowercase letters. • Recognize that spoken words are represented in written language by specific sequences of letters.
Fluency	• Read emergent-reader texts with purpose and understanding.
Phonics and Word Recognition	• Know and apply grade-level phonics and word-analysis skills in decoding words. • Read common high-frequency words by sight. • Recognize and read grade-appropriate words.

TESOL and WIDA Standards

In this book, the following English language development standards are met: Standard 1: English language learners communicate for social and instructional purposes within the school setting. Standard 2: English language learners communicate information, ideas, and concepts necessary for academic success in the content area of language arts.

Name: _____

I	see	the	a
black	**red**	**brown**	**tan**

Practice: the

I see the bear.

Directions: Read the words. Use the key to color the picture. Read the sentence. Circle the word *the* in the sentence.

Name: _____

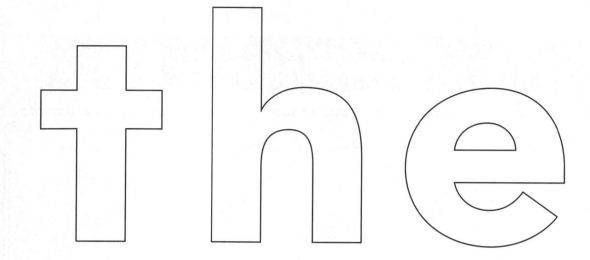

The  is ____ .

bike   pink

2

I like the ____ .

ice cream

3

Directions: Trace the word *the* with your finger at least 5 times, saying the name of each letter. Read the word. Color the word. Use the word in a sentence. Then, read the pages and circle the word *the* on each page.

no

of

go

of

am

of

of

of

of

up

the

of

of

of

a

me

so

Directions: Trace the word *of* with your finger at least 5 times, saying the name of each letter. Read the word. Use the word in a sentence. Find and circle the word *of*.

Name: _____

Directions: Trace the word *of* with your finger at least 5 times, saying the name of each letter. Read the word. Use the word in a sentence. Then, trace the words.

Name: _____

at _____ beach

lots _____ cats

over _____ moon

Directions: Trace the words *the* and *of*. Say the name of each letter as you do this. Read each word. Read the phrases. Write *the* or *of* to complete each phrase.

Name: _____

Can you find **and**?

b	v	o	a	n	d
a	n	d	p	u	x
c	e	w	a	n	d
y	a	n	d	w	k
r	u	a	n	d	o
a	n	d	s	j	r

Directions: Read the word *and*. Then, find and circle the word 6 times in the word search.

130219—180 Days of High-Frequency Words

Name: _____

Directions: Trace the word *and* with your finger at least 5 times, saying the name of each letter. Read the word. Use the word in a sentence. Cover the word with small objects. Color the word and the pictures. Then, go on a scavenger hunt to find this word in print.

Name: _____

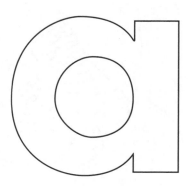

He has a

cape

4

She has a .

mask

5

Directions: Trace the word *a* with your finger at least 5 times. Read the word. Color the word. Use the word in a sentence. Then, read the pages and circle the word *a* on the pages of the book.

Name: _____

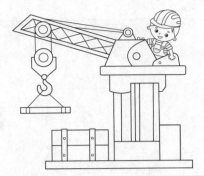

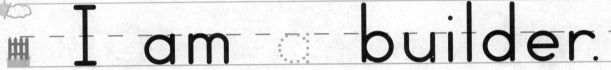
I am __ builder.

Do you see __ bike?

It is __ pig.

Directions: Write the word *a* in the sentences. Read the sentences. Color the pictures.

Name: _____

the

and

of

of

and

a

a

the

Directions: Read each word. Draw lines to match the words. Say each word in a sentence.

Name: _____

to

q	t	o	v	f	k
a	p	m	n	t	o
t	o	c	h	l	g
p	b	t	o	w	x

Directions: Read the word *to*. Find and circle the hidden word *to* 4 times. Tell a friend or adult where you like to go.

Name: _____

Words 1–10

Practice: to

We go to
a park.

To the bars
we go!

We run to
the swings.

Directions: Write the word *to* on the lines. Read the story. Talk about what you like to do at a park.

Name: _____

1. a puppy  _____ a house

2. children _____ the pool

3. a goldfish _____ a fishbowl

4. a bird _____ a nest

Directions: Write the word *in* to finish each phrase. Read the phrases. Name one object that is in another.

Name: _____

in   to

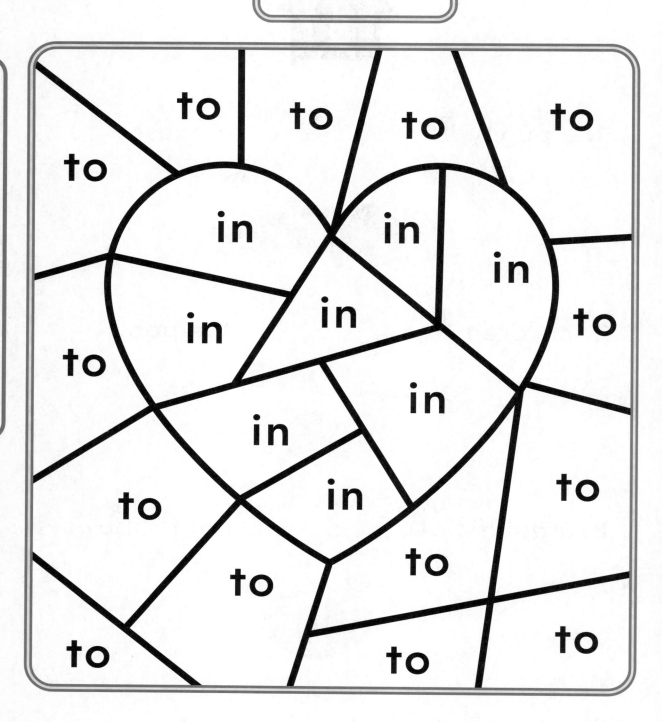

Directions: Color the spaces with *in* red. Color the spaces with *to* a different color. Tell a friend or adult what shape you see.

Name: _____

1

He put the gumball **in** his mouth.

2

He made a big bubble.

3

He went **to** the store.

Directions: Read each sentence. Draw lines to put the story in order. Color the pictures.

Name: _____

is	to	in	a
green	yellow	gray	black

It is a truck.

Directions: Read the words. Use the key to color the picture. Read the sentence. Circle the word *is* in the sentence.

Name: _____

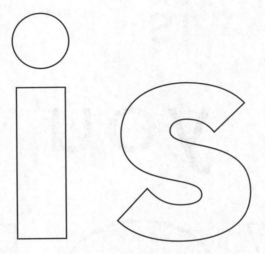

It is ● ●.
small

6

It is ● ●.
big

7

Directions: Trace the word *is* with your finger at least 5 times, saying the name of each letter. Read the word. Color the word. Use the word in a sentence. Then, read the pages and circle the word *is* on the pages of the book.

Name: _____

Words 1–10

Practice: you

a   is   you

you   you   of

you

you   in   you

of   the

a   in

you

and   to

Directions: Trace the word *you* with your finger at least 5 times, saying the name of each letter. Read the word. Use the word in a sentence. Find and circle the word *you*.

Name: _____

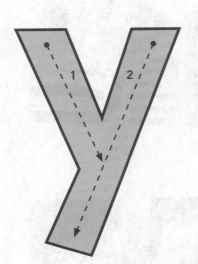 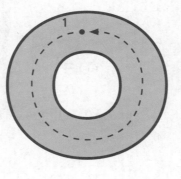 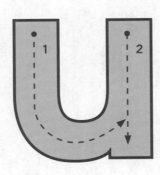

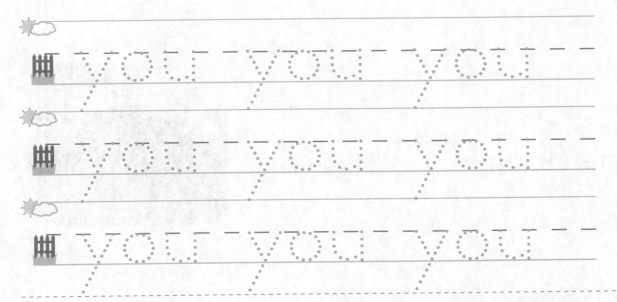

Directions: Trace the word *you* with your finger at least 5 times, saying the name of each letter. Read the word. Use the word in a sentence. Then, trace the words.

Name: _____

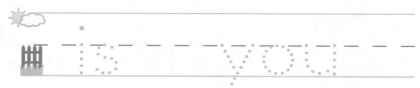

This  _____ me!

I see _____.

She _____ running.

Directions: Trace the words *is* and *you*. Say the name of each letter as you do this. Read each word. Read the sentences. Write *is* or *you* to complete each sentence.

Name: _____

Can you find **that**?

t	h	a	t	e	g
f	o	t	h	a	t
l	t	h	a	t	u
p	w	t	h	a	t
t	h	a	t	x	l
s	t	h	a	t	j

Practice: that   Words 1–10

Directions: Read the word *that*. Then, find and circle the word 6 times in the word search.

Name: _____

Directions: Trace the word *that* with your finger at least 5 times, saying the name of each letter. Read the word. Use the word in a sentence. Cover the word with small objects. Color the pictures. Then, go on a scavenger hunt to find this word in print.

Name: _____

It was .

frozen

8

Then, it  .

melted

9

Directions: Trace the word *it* with your finger at least 5 times, saying the name of each letter. Read the word. Color the word. Use the word in a sentence. Then, read the pages and circle the word *it* on the pages of the book.

Name: _____

Words 1–10

Practice: it

___ is a bug.

Do you see ___?

Is ___ a bug?

Directions: Write the word *it* in the sentences. Read the sentences. Color the pictures.

130219—180 Days of High-Frequency Words

Name: _____

is   that

you   you

that   it

it   is

Directions: Read each word. Draw lines to match the words. Say each word in a sentence.

Name: _____

the   of   and

Time to Draw

Directions: Draw and color your favorite place to go. Hide the words *and, of*, and *the* in your picture. Ask a friend or adult to find the hidden words.

Name: _____

the   of   and   a   to   in

A Day ☐☐ Movie Fun

I went ☐☐ see ☐ movie.

I got snacks ☐☐☐ a drink.

I went ☐☐ ☐☐☐ theater.

Time to Draw

Review: the, of, and   Words 1–10

Directions: Read the words and the story. Make the missing words by writing one letter in each box. Draw and color a picture for the story. Share it with a friend or adult.

Name: _____

is	you	that	it
red	yellow	brown	pink

Time to Draw

Directions: Read the words. Use the key to color the picture. Draw someone eating a bowl of ice cream. Share it with a friend or adult.

130219—180 Days of High-Frequency Words

Name: _____

is   you   that   it

Materials

- 2 or more players
- *High-Frequency Word Memory Game Cards 1–10* (page 43)

Directions: Place the cut-out *High-Frequency Word Memory Game Cards* facedown on the game board. Take turns. Turn over 2 cards at a time to make word matches. Keep the matches you find. Play until you find all the matches.

Name: _____

the	and	to	is	that
of	a	in	you	it

Materials

- 2 players
- pencils and crayons (1 color per player)
- *High-Frequency Word Cards 1–10* (page 207)
- 1 number cube

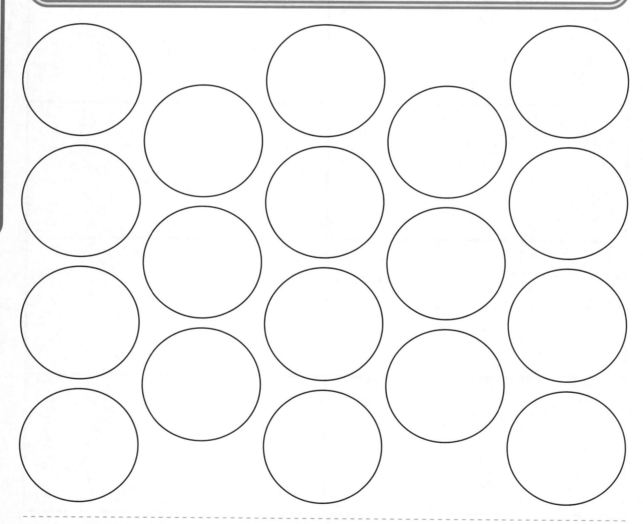

Directions: Put the cut-out *High-Frequency Word Cards* facedown in a pile. The first player rolls the number cube and chooses a card. Then, they write the word in a circle and color the number of circles on the cube. Players take turns until all circles are colored. The player with the most colored circles wins.

High-Frequency Word Memory
Game Cards 1–10

is

is

you

you

that

that

it

it

High-Frequency Word
Memory Game Cards
1–10

High-Frequency Word
Memory Game Cards
1–10

High-Frequency Word
Memory Game Cards
1–10

High-Frequency Word
Memory Game Cards
1–10

High-Frequency Word
Memory Game Cards
1–10

High-Frequency Word
Memory Game Cards
1–10

High-Frequency Word
Memory Game Cards
1–10

High-Frequency Word
Memory Game Cards
1–10

Name: _____

he

Words 11–20

Practice: he

q b h e f k

h e m n g a

r u d i h e

s h e v j y

Directions: Read the word *he*. Find and circle the hidden word *he* 4 times.

Name: _____

He can go fast.

Can he go?

We see he can go up and down.

Directions: Write the word *he* on the lines. Read the story. Tell about another activity he can do.

Name: _____

1. A dog's tail _____ wagging.

2. A child _____ smiling.

3. A pig _____ in the mud.

4. A cat _____ playing.

Directions: Write the word *was* to finish each sentence. Read the sentences. Color the pictures.

Name: _____

Words 11–20   Practice: was

he   was

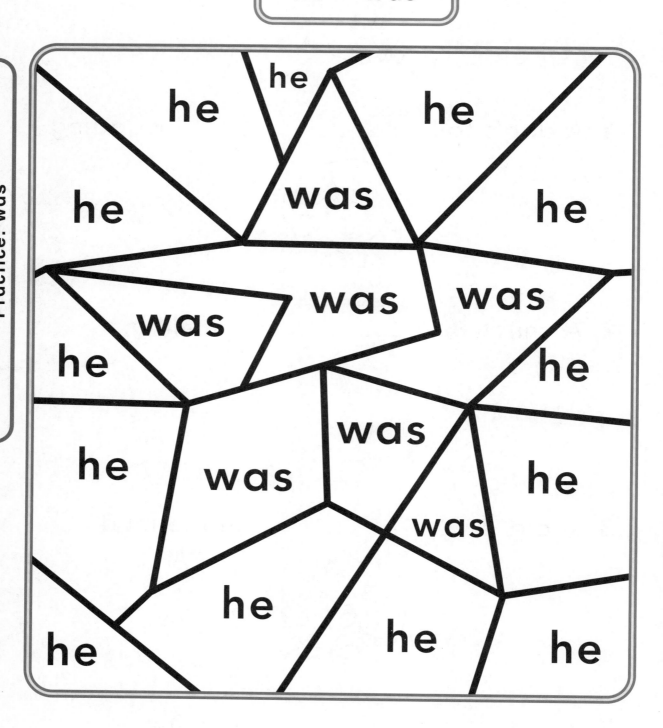

Directions: Color the spaces with *was* yellow. Color the spaces with *he* a different color. Tell a friend or adult what shape you see.

Name: _____

1

2

3

He went to swim.

Then, **he** got to swim.

He put on floaties. **He was** ready!

Directions: Read each sentence. Draw lines to put the story in order. Color the pictures.

Name: _____

he	was	it	for
red	orange	yellow	blue

It looks for the sun.

Directions: Read the words. Use the key to color the picture. Read the sentence. Circle the word *for* in the sentence.

Name: _____

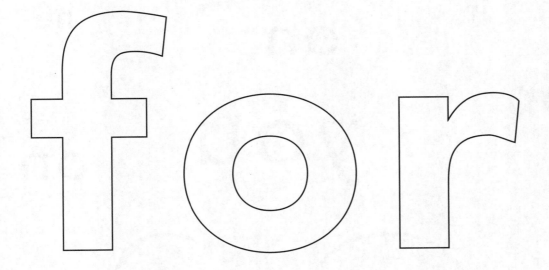

It is a 🛴 for you.
scooter
10

It is a 👑 for you.
crown
11

Directions: Trace the word *for* with your finger at least 5 times, saying the name of each letter. Read the word. Color the word. Use the word in a sentence. Then, read the pages and circle the word *for* on the pages of the book.

Name: _____

it

on

he

on

you

on

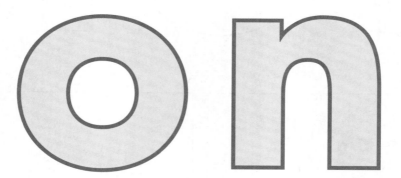

in

that

on

was

to

a

on

and

on

Directions: Trace the word *on* with your finger at least 5 times, saying the name of each letter. Read the word. Use the word in a sentence. Find and circle the word *on*.

Name: _____

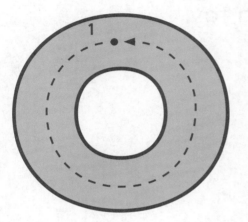 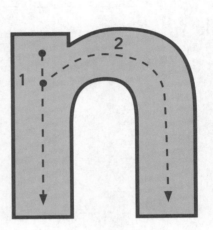

Directions: Trace the word *on* with your finger at least 5 times, saying the name of each letter. Read the word. Use the word in a sentence. Then, write the words.

Name: _____

for on

Look _____ a toy.

Sit _____ that.

It is lunch _____ us.

Directions: Trace the words *for* and *on*. Say the name of each letter as you do this. Read each word. Read the sentences. Write *for* or *on* to complete each sentence. Color the pictures.

Name: _____

Can you find **are**?

k	s	p	a	r	e
b	a	r	e	i	s
x	o	a	r	e	g
g	b	l	a	r	e
a	r	e	i	t	h
s	a	r	e	o	y

Directions: Read the word *are*. Then, find and circle the word 6 times in the word search.

We are a team.

are

We are sisters.   We are twins.

Directions: Trace the word *are* with your finger at least 5 times, saying the name of each letter. Read the word. Use the word in a sentence. Cover the word with small objects. Color the word and the pictures. Then, go on a scavenger hunt to find this word in print.

a s

brown as a
bear

12

brown as a
moth

13

Directions: Trace the word *as* with your finger at least 5 times, saying the name of each letter. Read the word. Color the word. Use the word in a sentence. Then, read the pages and circle the word *as* on the pages of the book.

Name: _____

small as an ant

tall as a giraffe

big as a whale

Directions: Write the word *as* in each sentence. Read the sentences. Color the pictures.

130219—180 Days of High-Frequency Words

Name: _____

for

on

are

as

are

for

as

on

Directions: Read each word. Draw lines to match the words. Say each word in a sentence.

Practice: with

Name: _____

with

w i t h f k

a b w i t h

e w i t h g

w i t h l m

Directions: Read the word *with*. Find and circle the hidden word *with* 4 times. Tell a friend or adult who you like to play with outside.

130219—180 Days of High-Frequency Words

© Shell Education

Name: _____

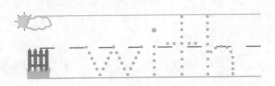

May I go  _____ you?

I like to go _____ you.

I will go in _____ you.

Directions: Write the word *with* on the lines. Then, color the pictures. Talk about who you like to go with on adventures.

Name: _____

1. in _____ yard

2. with _____ dad

3. by _____ dog

4. with _____ toy

Directions: Write the word *his* on the lines. Read the phrases. Color the pictures.

his   with

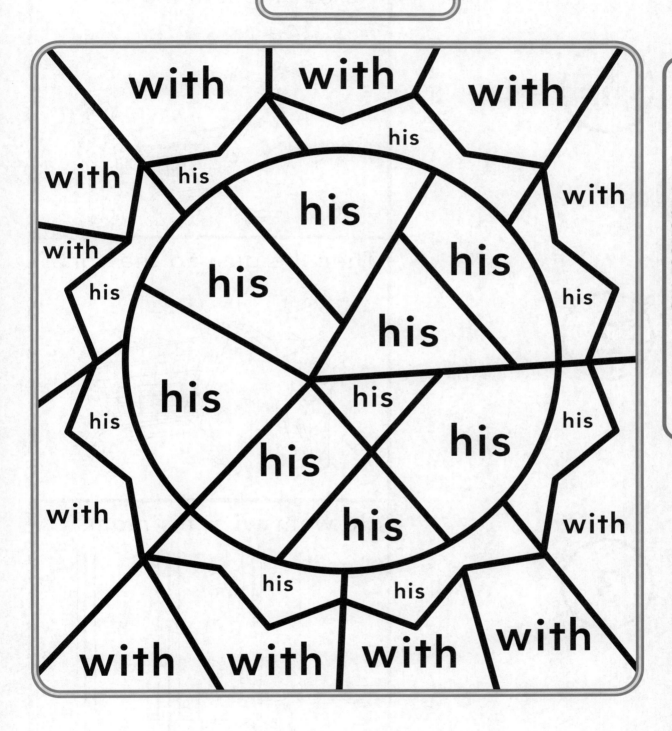

Directions: Color the spaces with *his* yellow. Color the spaces that have *with* a different color. Tell a friend or adult what you see.

Words 11–20

Review: with, his

1

2

3

He put them in **his** cart.

Then, he pushed the cart.

He went **with** his mom.

Directions: Read the story. Draw lines to put the story in order. Color the pictures.

Name: _____

they	with	his	as
pink	green	yellow	blue

They are flowers.

Directions: Read the words. Use the key to color the picture. Read the sentence. Circle the word *they* in the sentence.

Name: _____

Words 11–20

Practice: they

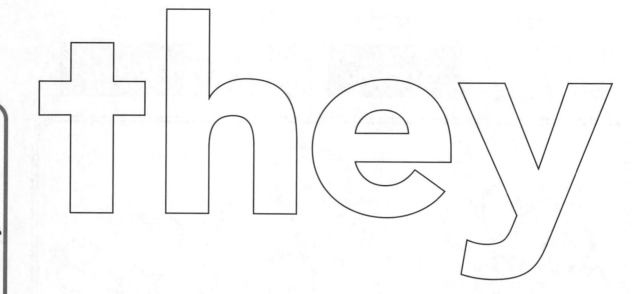

They are in .

snow

14

They are in _____.

water

15

Directions: Trace the word *they* with your finger at least 5 times, saying the name of each letter. Read the word. Color the word. Use the word in a sentence. Then, read the pages and circle the word *they* on the pages of the book.

Name: _____

for

one

I

I

are

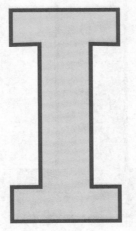

was

I

that

you

in

I

is

it

I

I

he

Directions: Trace the word *I* with your finger at least 5 times, saying the name of the letter. Read the word. Use the word in a sentence. Find and circle the word *I*.

Name: _____

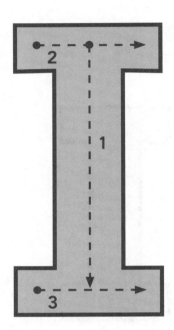

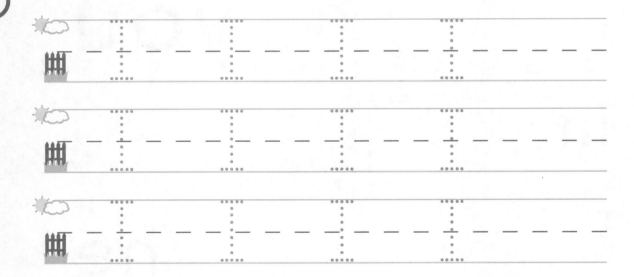

Directions: Trace the word *I* with your finger at least 5 times. Read the word. Use the word in a sentence. Then, write the words.

Name: _____

they I

Are _____ ready?

_____ are happy.

_____ am ready.

Directions: Trace the words *they* and *I*. Say the name of each letter as you do this. Read each word. Read the sentences. Write *they* or *I* to complete each sentence.

© Shell Education

130219—180 Days of High-Frequency Words

Words 11–20

Review: he, was, for

Name: _____

he   was   for

Time to Draw

Directions: Draw and color your favorite room in a home. Hide the words *he, was,* and *for* inside your picture. Ask a friend or adult to find the hidden words.

Name: _____

He   for   on   are   as

The Farm

A boy is ☐☐ the farm.

Pigs are in the mud, ☐☐ dirty ☐☐ can be.

☐ looks ☐☐ horses.

Where ☐☐☐ the cows?

Directions: Read the words and the story. Make the missing words by writing one letter in each box. One word is used twice. Read the story with an adult.

Name: _____

with	this	they	I
red	yellow	blue	green

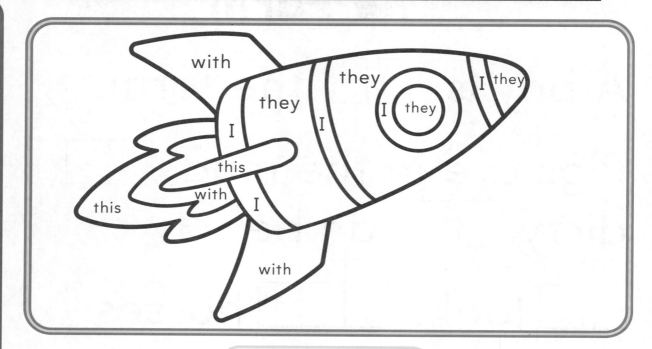

Time to Draw

Directions: Read the words. Use the key to color the picture. Draw a picture of outer space. Share it with a friend or adult.

130219—180 Days of High-Frequency Words

© Shell Education

Name: _____

| with | his | they | I |

Materials

- 2 or more players
- *High-Frequency Word Memory Game Cards 11–20* (page 75)

Directions: Place the cut-out *High-Frequency Word Memory Game Cards* facedown on the game board. Take turns. Turn over 2 cards at a time to make word matches. Keep the matches you find. Play until you find all the matches.

Name: _____

he	for	are	with	they
was	on	as	his	I

Materials

- 2 players
- 1 number cube
- pencils and crayons (1 color per player)
- *High-Frequency Word Cards 11–20* (page 209)

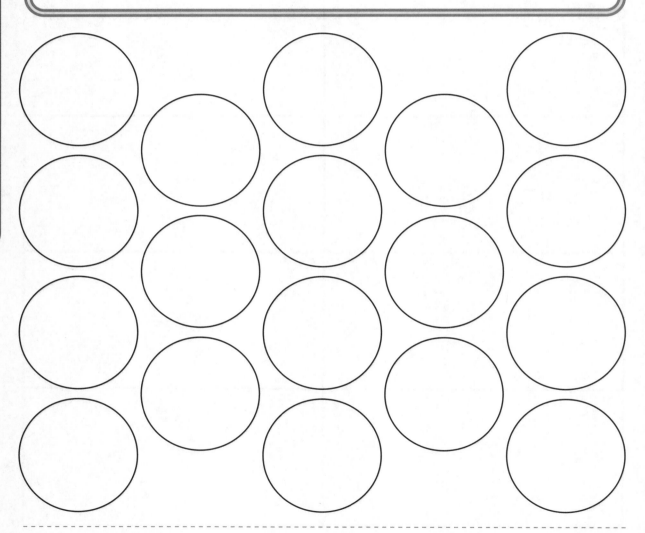

Directions: Put the cut-out *High-Frequency Word Cards 11–20* facedown in a pile. The first player rolls the number cube and chooses a card. Then, they write the word in a circle and color the number of circles on the cube. Players take turns until all circles are colored. The player with the most colored circles wins.

High-Frequency Word Memory Game Cards 11–20

with	with
his	his
they	they
I	I

High-Frequency Word
Memory Game Cards
11–20

High-Frequency Word
Memory Game Cards
11–20

High-Frequency Word
Memory Game Cards
11–20

High-Frequency Word
Memory Game Cards
11–20

High-Frequency Word
Memory Game Cards
11–20

High-Frequency Word
Memory Game Cards
11–20

High-Frequency Word
Memory Game Cards
11–20

High-Frequency Word
Memory Game Cards
11–20

Name: _____

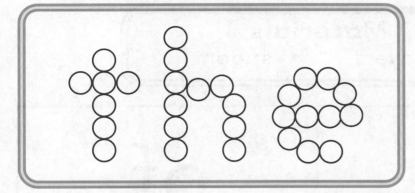

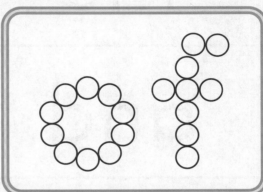

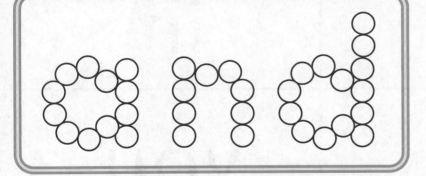

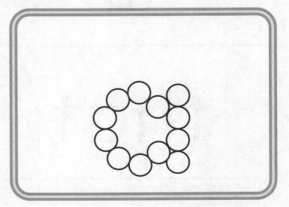

Directions: Read the words *the, of, and,* and *a.* Color or paint the circles to make the letters for each word. Use the words in sentences. Share the sentences with a friend or adult.

Name: _____

Materials
- 2 players
- spoon

the	of
and	a
to	in
is	you
that	it

Directions: Read the words with a friend or adult. One player reads the words in any order, while the other player taps the words with a spoon. See how many words you can read and tap in 1 minute.

Name: _____

Directions: Read the words with an adult. In a dark room, use a flashlight to trace the letters with light. Then, color the words.

Cumulative Review of Words 1–20

I Know 20 Words!

Name: _____

the
and
to
is
that

the	◯ ◯ ◯ ◯ ◯ ◯ ◯
and	◯ ◯ ◯ ◯ ◯ ◯ ◯
to	◯ ◯ ◯ ◯ ◯ ◯ ◯
is	◯ ◯ ◯ ◯ ◯ ◯ ◯
that	◯ ◯ ◯ ◯ ◯ ◯ ◯

Directions: Read the words *the, and, to, is,* and *that* with a friend or adult. Find a book or magazine. Search for the words in the text. Color one circle each time you see one of the words. Tell which word you see the most.

Name: _____

Words with *a*	Words with *e*	Words with *i*	Words with *o*
red	yellow	blue	green

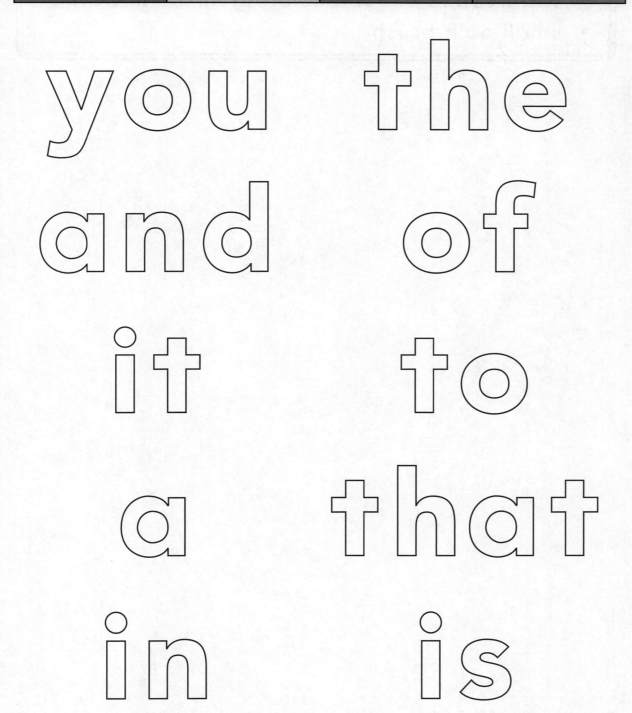

you the

and of

it to

a that

in is

Directions: Read the words. Use the key to color the words. Make the words with dough.

Name: _____

Materials

- white or light-colored crayon
- watercolors or food coloring mixed in water
- small paintbrush

Directions: Write 5 high-frequency words you know with a white or light-colored crayon. Use watercolors (or food coloring with a small amount of water) to paint over each word. Read the words that pop out.

Name: _____

Directions: Trace and read the words. Color the hopscotch game. With an adult or friend, use chalk to make this hopscotch plan and play hopscotch outside.

Name: _____

Materials
- 2 players
- 2 different-colored crayons
- coin

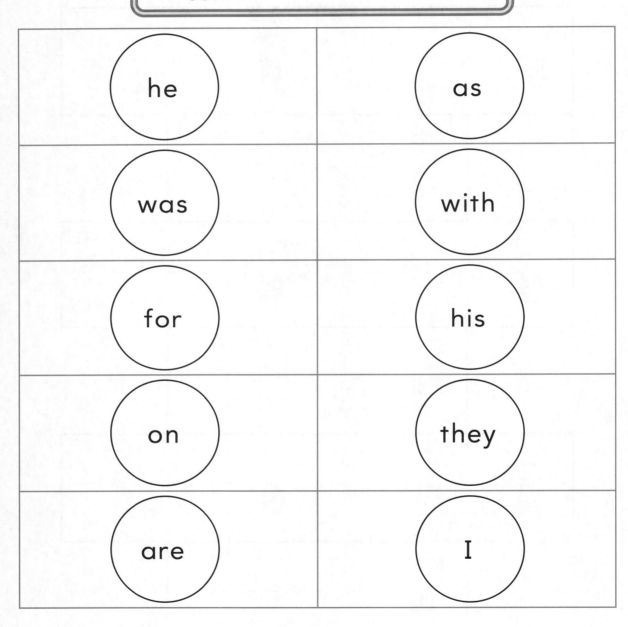

he	as
was	with
for	his
on	they
are	I

Directions: Read the words. Choose a color. Take turns flipping the coin onto the page. If the coin lands on a circle, read the word in the circle and color the circle. Play until all the circles are colored. The player with the most colored circles wins.

Name: _____

he	for	are	with	they
was	on	as	his	I

Directions: Read the words. Find and circle these words hidden in the picture. Color the picture.

Cumulative Review of Words 1–20

I Know 20 Words!

Name: _____

Materials

- 2 or more players
- Word Jar with *High-Frequency Word Cards 1–20*

the	of	and	a	to
in	is	you	that	it
he	was	for	on	are
as	with	his	they	I

Directions: Read the words. Make sure all 20 words are in your Word Jar. Shake some word cards out of your Word Jar onto a table. Read the words that face up. Repeat and take turns with other players.

Name: _____

Can you find **at**?

w	a	t	g	u	c
a	t	f	s	m	r
u	c	d	k	a	t
a	t	o	b	n	d
y	p	a	t	w	h
z	f	k	a	t	q

Directions: Read the word *at*. Then, find and circle the word 6 times in the word search.

Name: _____

Directions: Trace the word *at* with your finger at least 5 times, saying the name of each letter. Read the word. Use the word in a sentence. Cover the word with small objects. Color the word and the pictures. Then, go on a scavenger hunt to find this word in print.

Name: _____

be

Be  to a  .
kind   friend

16

You can be 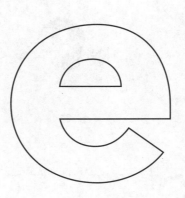 .
kind

17

Directions: Trace the word *be* with your finger at least 5 times, saying the name of each letter. Read the word. Color the word. Use the word in a sentence. Then, read the pages and circle the word *be* on the pages of the book.

Name: _____

to be brave

to be kind

to be strong

Directions: Trace the word *be*. Read the phrases. Color the picture.

130219—180 Days of High-Frequency Words   © Shell Education

at

be

At

Be

be

At

Be

at

Directions: Read each word. Draw lines to match the words. Say each word in a sentence.

Name: _____

Words 21–30

Practice: this

this

a t h i s e

t h i s f g

t h i s l m

o n t h i s

Directions: Read the word *this*. Find and circle the hidden word *this* 4 times. Tell a friend or adult what your favorite high-frequency word is.

Name: _____

1. Do you like  _____ one?

2. I like _____ color.

3. We both like _____.

Time to Draw

Directions: Write the word *this* to finish the story. Read the story. Draw with your favorite marker colors.

Name: _____

1. We  _____ treats.

2. They _____ a snack.

3. She can _____ it.

4. He can _____ it.

Directions: Write the word *have* to finish each sentence. Read the sentences. Color the pictures. Tell about a treat you like to have.

Name: _____

have   this

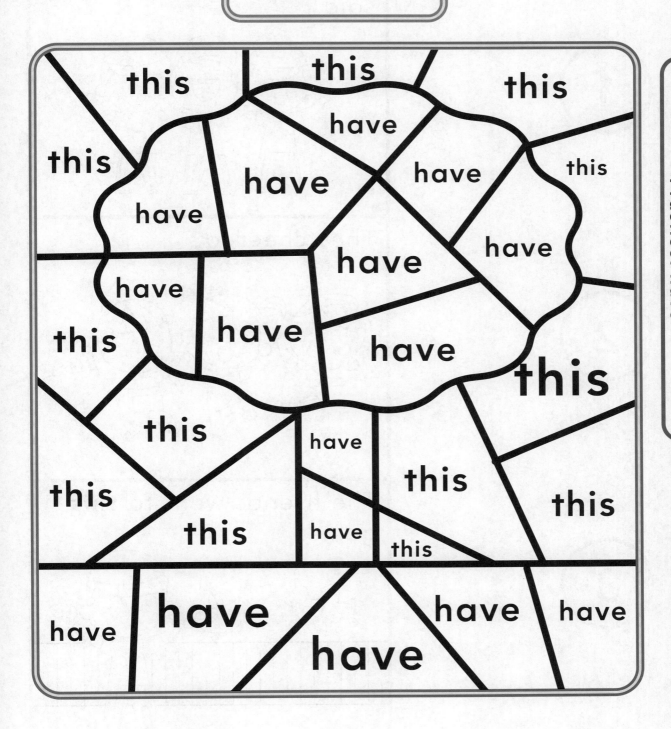

Directions: Color the spaces with *have* green. Color the spaces with *this* blue. Tell a friend or adult what you see.

Name: _____

1

"We **have** won **this**!" they said.

2

They cheered.

3

The friends went to **this** game.

Directions: Read each sentence. Draw lines to put the story in order. Color the pictures.

Name: _____

from	this	have	be
blue	**brown**	**black**	**red**

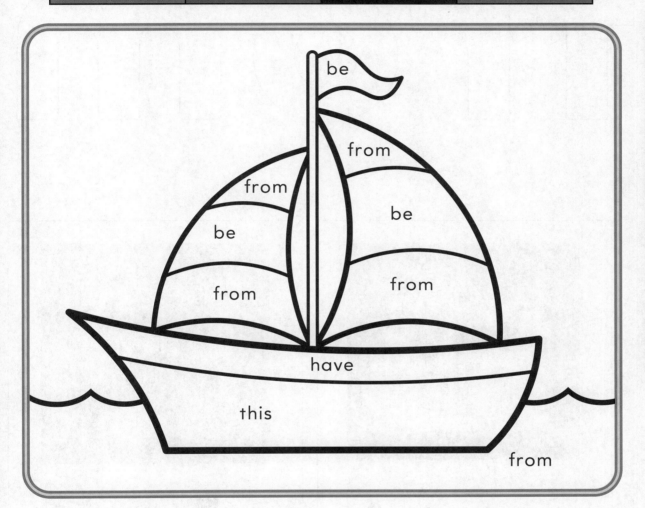

This came from the ocean.

Directions: Read the words. Use the key to color the picture. Read the sentence. Circle the word *from* in the sentence.

Name: _____

from

This 🎂 is from 👩.
cake   mom
18

This 🧸 is from 👨.
bear   dad
19

Directions: Trace the word *from* with your finger at least 5 times, saying the name of each letter. Read the word. Color the word. Use the word in a sentence. Then, read the pages and circle the word *from* on the pages of the book.

Name: _____

Words 21–30

Practice: or

he

or

or

or

for

was

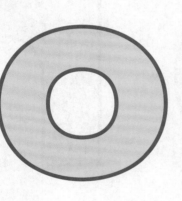 

I

that

are

on

with

his

it

or

I

or

they

Directions: Trace the word *or* with your finger at least 5 times, saying the name of each letter. Read the word. Use the word in a sentence. Find and circle the word *or*.

Name: _____

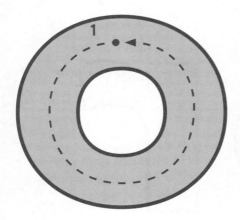 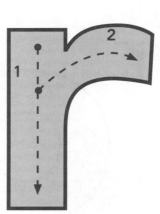

Directions: Trace the word *or* at least 5 times with your finger, saying the name of each letter. Read the word. Use the word in a sentence. Then, trace the words.

130219—180 Days of High-Frequency Words   © Shell Education

Name: _____

from   or

He came _____ the bus.

Do you like dogs _____ cats?

I see a note _____ my grandpa.

Directions: Trace the words *from* and *or*. Say the name of each letter as you do this. Read each word. Read the sentences. Write *from* or *or* to complete each sentence.

Name: _____

Can you find **one**?

l	e	p	o	n	e
f	s	j	o	n	e
c	f	o	n	e	d
o	n	e	d	u	t
r	o	n	e	k	a
s	m	o	n	e	r

Directions: Read the word *one*. Then, find and circle the word 6 times in the word search.

© Shell Education

Name: _____

Directions: Trace the word *one* with your finger at least 5 times, saying the name of each letter. Read the word. Use the word in a sentence. Cover the word with small objects. Color the word and the pictures. Then, go on a scavenger hunt to find this word in print.

Name: _____

I had  .
carrots

I had .
grapes

20

I had . MILK
milk

I had .
lunch

21

Directions: Trace the word *had* with your finger at least 5 times, saying the name of each letter. Read the word. Color the word. Use the word in a sentence. Then, read the pages and circle the word *had* on the pages of the book.

Name: _____

had

I had my nap.

We had fun together.

We had a laugh.

Directions: Trace the word *had* in the sentences. Read each sentence. Color the pictures.

Name: _____

One

had

one

Had

had

One

Had

one

Directions: Read each word. Draw lines to match the words. Say each word in a sentence.

Name: _____

by

b y a c b e

l m b y s d

t h o n b y

j k h b y s

Directions: Read the word *by*. Find and circle the hidden word *by* 4 times. Tell a friend or adult what your favorite high-frequency word is.

Name: _____

1. She is _____ her mom.

2. They walk _____ the pet store.

3. Next, they walk _____ a toy store.

4. Then, they walk _____ a friend's house.

Directions: Write the word *by* in each sentence to finish the story. Read the sentences. Talk about what you like to walk by.

Name: _____

1. Some  _____
have 2 letters.

2. Other  _____
have 3 letters.

3. Some _____
have more.

4. _____

Directions: Write the word *words* to finish each sentence. Read the sentences. Color the pictures. Write some words you know.

Name: _____

words   by

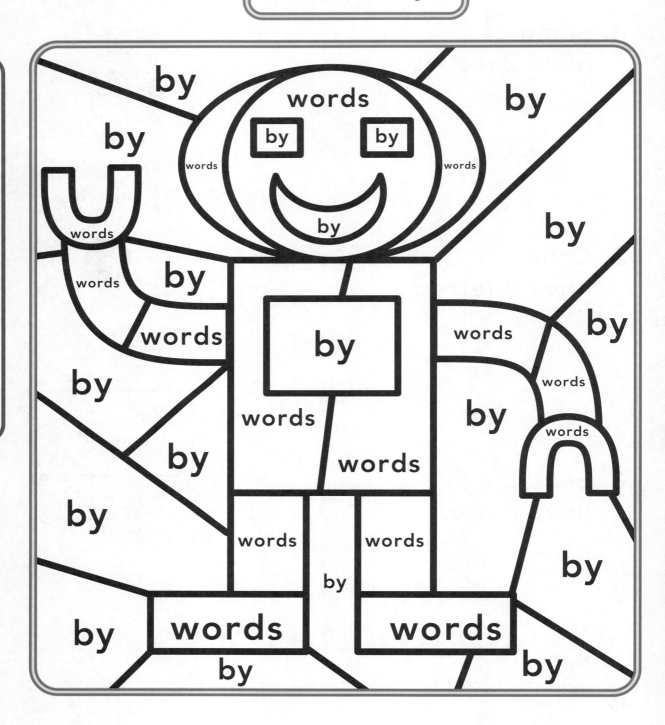

Directions: Color the spaces with *words* red. Color the spaces with *by* yellow. Tell a friend or adult what you see.

Name: _____

1

2

3

I went **by** the park.

We read the **words** on the sign.

Be Safe

I saw a friend **by** the tables.

Directions: Read each sentence. Draw lines to put the story in order. Color the pictures.

Name: _____

at   be   this

Time to Draw

Directions: Draw and color your favorite place to play. Hide the words *at, be*, and *this* inside your picture. Ask a friend or adult to find the hidden words.

at   be   this   have   from   or

At the Lake

A girl was ⬚⬚ the lake.

She knew ⬚⬚⬚ the

sunshine ⬚⬚⬚ was going

to ⬚⬚ a nice day.

Do I ⬚⬚⬚ my big hat, ⬚⬚

do I need an umbrella?

Directions: Read the words and the story. Make the missing words by writing one letter in each box. Draw a picture for the story on another sheet of paper. Share it with a friend or adult.

Name: _____

one	had	by	words
red	yellow	blue	green

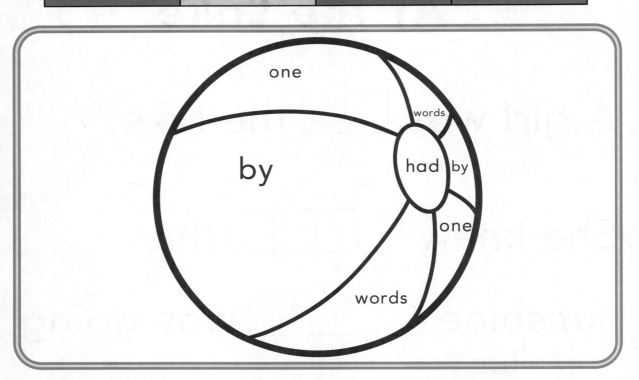

Time to Draw

Directions: Read the words. Use the key to color the picture. Draw yourself playing with a beach ball. Share it with a friend or adult.

Name: _____

one   had   by   words

Materials

- 2 or more players
- *High-Frequency Word Memory Game Cards 21–30* (page 117)

Directions: Place the cut-out *High-Frequency Word Memory Game Cards* facedown on the game board. Take turns. Turn over 2 cards at a time to make word matches. Keep the matches you find. Play until you find all the matches.

Words 21–30 | **Review**

Name: _____

| at | this | from | one | by |
| be | have | or | had | words |

Materials

- 2 players
- 1 number cube
- pencils and crayons (1 color per player)
- *High-Frequency Word Cards 21–30* (page 211)

Directions: Put the cut-out *High-Frequency Word Cards* facedown in a pile. The first player rolls the number cube and chooses a card. Then, they write the word in a circle and color the number of circles on the cube. Players take turns until all circles are colored. The player with the most colored circles wins.

High-Frequency Word Memory
Game Cards 21–30

one	one
had	had
by	by
words	words

High-Frequency Word
Memory Game Cards
21–30

High-Frequency Word
Memory Game Cards
21–30

High-Frequency Word
Memory Game Cards
21–30

High-Frequency Word
Memory Game Cards
21–30

High-Frequency Word
Memory Game Cards
21–30

High-Frequency Word
Memory Game Cards
21–30

High-Frequency Word
Memory Game Cards
21–30

High-Frequency Word
Memory Game Cards
21–30

one	had	by	but
gray	yellow	black	red

She is ready, but there is no fire.

Directions: Read the words. Use the key to color the picture. Read the sentence. Circle the word *but* in the sentence.

Words 31–40

Practice: but

Name: _____

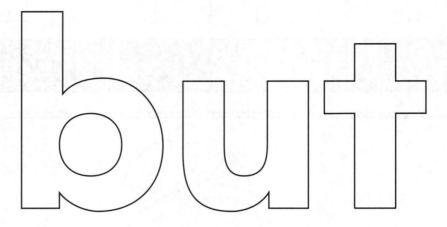

This is ○● but 😞 .
small   warm

22

These are ○●
small

but 🏃 .
fast

23

Directions: Trace the word *but* with your finger at least 5 times, saying the name of each letter. Read the word. Color the word. Use the word in a sentence. Then, read the pages and circle the word *but* on the pages of the book.

Name: _____

be

not

this

have

not

not

from

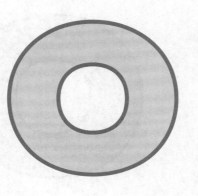

one

words

had

not

not

by

or

I

not

but

Directions: Trace the word *not* with your finger at least 5 times, saying the name of each letter. Read the word. Use the word in a sentence. Find and circle the word *not*.

Name: _____

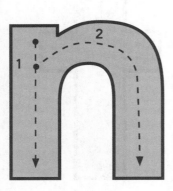 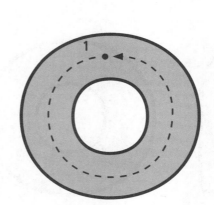 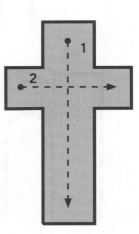

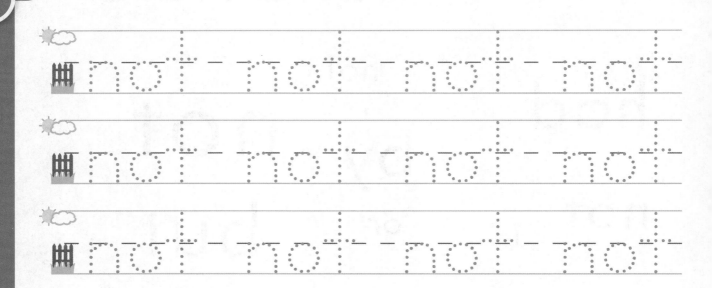

Directions: Trace the word *not* with your finger at least 5 times, saying the name of each letter. Read the word. Use the word in a sentence. Then, trace the words.

Name: _____

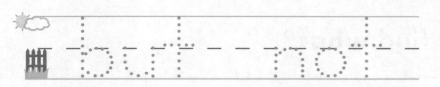

Do you like it or _____ ?

She had it, _____ there was no rain.

I am _____ the baby now.

Directions: Trace the words *but* and *not*. Say the name of each letter as you do this. Read each word. Read the sentences. Write *but* or *not* to complete each sentence.

Name: _____

Can you find **what**?

o	w	h	a	t	d
k	n	w	h	a	t
w	h	a	t	j	s
y	i	w	h	a	t
c	w	h	a	t	u
w	h	a	t	j	f

Directions: Read the word *what*. Then, find and circle the word 6 times in the word search.

Name: _____

Directions: Trace the word *what* with your finger at least 5 times, saying the name of each letter. Read the word. Use the word in a sentence. Cover the word with small objects. Color the word and the pictures. Then, go on a scavenger hunt to find this word in print.

Name: _____

all

We are all at the  .
movies

24

We are all at the 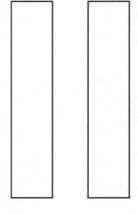 .
park

25

Directions: Trace the word *all* with your finger at least 5 times, saying the name of each letter. Read the word. Color the word. Use the word in a sentence. Then, read the pages and circle the word *all* on the pages of the book.

Name: _____

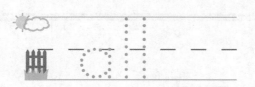

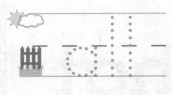 my friends

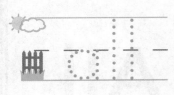 together

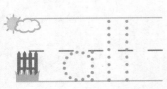 aboard

Directions: Trace the word *all* in the phrases. Read the phrases. Color the pictures.

Name: _____

what

all

What

What

All

what

all

All

Directions: Read each word. Draw lines to match the words. Say each word in a sentence.

were	what	all	not
brown	tan	pink	yellow

They were eating bananas.

Directions: Read the words. Use the key to color the picture. Read the sentence. Circle the word *were* in the sentence.

Name: _____

were

We were at the  .

zoo

26

We were at the  .

store

27

Directions: Trace the word *were* with your finger at least 5 times, saying the name of each letter. Read the word. Color the word. Use the word in a sentence. Then, read the pages and circle the word *were* on the pages of the book.

Name: _____

or

we

we

we

had

but

we

one

not

what

we

all

we

we

were

Directions: Trace the word *we* with your finger at least 5 times, saying the name of each letter. Read the word. Use the word in a sentence. Find and circle the word *we*.

Name: _____

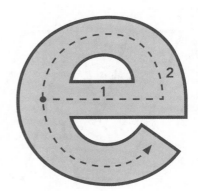

we we we we

we we we we

we we we we

Directions: Trace the word *we* with your finger at least 5 times, saying the name of each letter. Read the word. Use the word in a sentence. Then, trace the words.

Name: _____

They _____ fast.

Do _____ hear it?

Yes, _____ went to a movie.

Directions: Trace the words *were* and *we*. Say the name of each letter as you do this. Read each word. Read the sentences. Write *were* or *we* to complete each sentence.

Words 31–40

Practice: when

Name: _____

Can you find **when**?

w	h	e	n	v	g
f	r	w	h	e	n
c	w	h	e	n	d
u	l	w	h	e	n
w	h	e	n	k	b
s	w	h	e	n	r

Directions: Read the word *when*. Then, find and circle the word 6 times in the word search.

130219—180 Days of High-Frequency Words

Name: _____

when

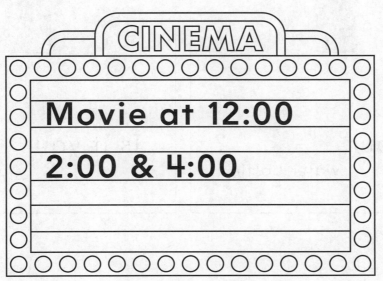

CINEMA

Movie at 12:00

2:00 & 4:00

Directions: Trace the word *when* with your finger at least 5 times, saying the name of each letter. Read the word. Use the word in a sentence. Cover the word with small objects. Color the word and the pictures. Then, go on a scavenger hunt to find this word in print.

Name: _____

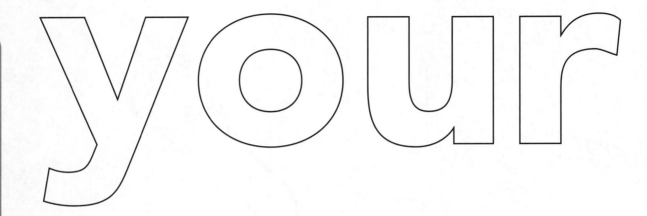

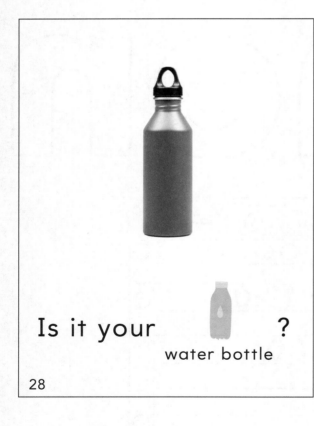

Is it your ?

water bottle

28

Is it your  ?

lunchbox

29

Directions: Trace the word *your* with your finger at least 5 times, saying the name of each letter. Read the word. Color the word. Use the word in a sentence. Then, read the pages and circle the word *your* on the pages of the book.

Name: _____

 your mom and dad

your uniform

your room

Directions: Trace the word *your* in the phrases. Read the phrases. Color the pictures.

Name: _____

when   When

Your   when

your   Your

When   your

Directions: Read each word. Draw lines to match the words. Say each word in a sentence.

130219—180 Days of High-Frequency Words

Name: _____

can

c a n e f k
a o m c a n
b c a n l g
p h c a n x

Directions: Read the word *can*. Find and circle the word *can* 4 times. Tell a friend or adult what you can do.

Name: _____

1. We  _____ swing.

2. _____ we jump?

3. We _____ play.

4. We _____ slide.

Directions: Write the word *can* in the sentences. Read the sentences. Color the pictures. Tell about how you can play.

Name: _____

Words 31—40

Practice: said

1. They  _____
hello.

2. We _____
goodbye.

3. He  _____
thank you.

4. She _____
I love you.

Directions: Write the word *said* to finish each sentence. Read the sentences. Color the pictures.

Name: _____

said   can

Directions: Color the spaces with *said* purple. Color the spaces with *can* green. Tell a friend or adult what you see and whether you like to eat these.

130219—180 Days of High-Frequency Words   © Shell Education

Name: _____

1

2

3

"We **can** both do this," they **said**.

"I **can** do this, too," he **said**.

"I **can** do this," she **said**.

Directions: Read each sentence. Draw lines to put the story in order. Color the pictures.

Words 31–40

Review: but, not, what

Name: _____

but   not   what

Time to Draw

Directions: Draw and color your favorite animals in the wild. Hide the words *but, not,* and *what* inside your picture. Ask a friend or adult to find the hidden words.

Name: _____

| but | not | What | All | were | We |

Review: but, not, what, all, were, we

Words 31–40

Camping

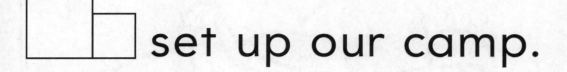 set up our camp.

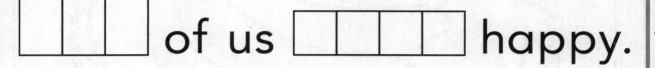 of us ⬚⬚⬚ happy.

It was cold, ⬚⬚ we kept warm.

 a campfire we made!

We love camping and do ⬚⬚ want to go home.

Directions: Read the words and the story. Make the missing words by writing one letter in each box. Draw a picture for the story on another sheet of paper. Share it with a friend or adult.

Name: _____

we	when	your	can	said
red	yellow	green	orange	blue

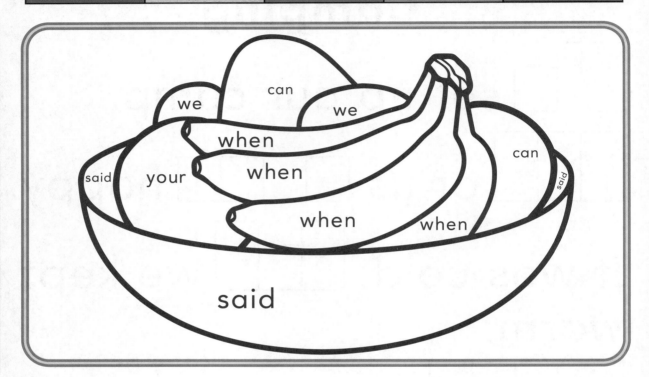

Time to Draw

Directions: Read the words. Use the key to color the picture. Draw your favorite fruit. Share it with a friend or adult.

Name: _____

when   your   can   said

Materials

- 2 or more players
- *High-Frequency Word Memory Game Cards 31–40* (page 149)

Directions: Place the cut-out *High-Frequency Word Memory Game Cards* facedown on the game board. Take turns. Turn over 2 cards at a time to make word matches. Keep the matches you find. Play until you find all the matches.

Name: _____

| but | what | were | when | can |
| not | all | your | said | we |

Materials

- 2 players
- 1 number cube
- pencils and crayons (1 color per player)
- *High-Frequency Word Cards 31–40* (page 213)

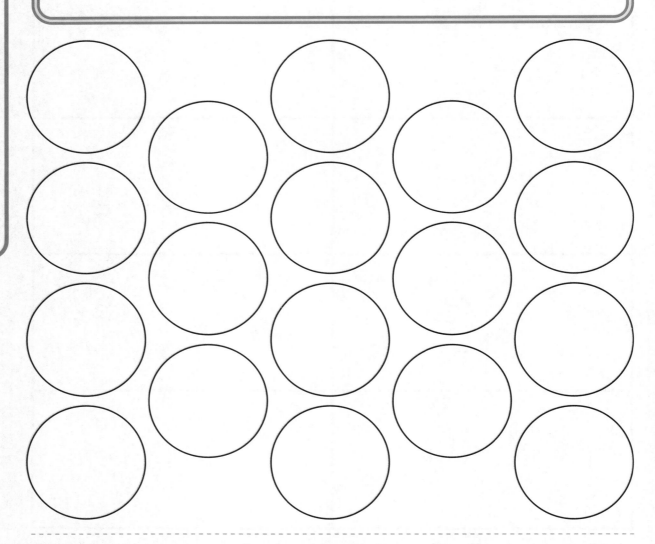

Directions: Put the cut-out *High-Frequency Word Cards* facedown in a pile. The first player rolls the number cube and chooses a card. Then, they write the word in a circle and color the number of circles on the cube. Players take turns until all circles are colored. The player with the most colored circles wins.

High-Frequency Word Memory Game Cards 31–40

when	when
your	your
can	can
said	said

High-Frequency Word
Memory Game Cards
31–40

High-Frequency Word
Memory Game Cards
31–40

High-Frequency Word
Memory Game Cards
31–40

High-Frequency Word
Memory Game Cards
31–40

High-Frequency Word
Memory Game Cards
31–40

High-Frequency Word
Memory Game Cards
31–40

High-Frequency Word
Memory Game Cards
31–40

High-Frequency Word
Memory Game Cards
31–40

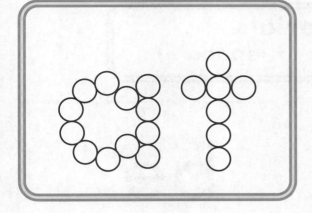

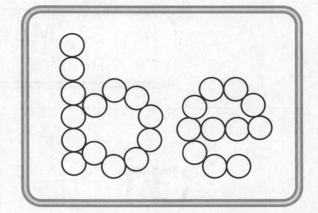

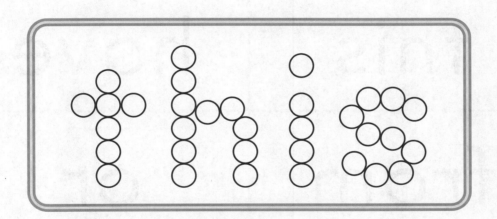

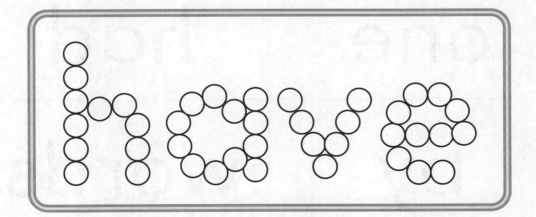

Directions: Read the words *at, be, this,* and *have.* Color or paint the circles to make the letters for each word. Use the words in sentences. Share the sentences with a friend or adult.

Name: _____

Materials
- 2 players
- spoon

at	be
this	have
from	or
one	had
by	words

Directions: Read the words with a friend or adult. One player reads the words in any order, while the other player taps the words with a spoon. See how many words you can read and tap in 1 minute.

Name: _____

at

or

be

one

this

had

have

by

from

words

Directions: Read the words with an adult. In a dark room, use a flashlight to trace the letters with light. Then, color the words.

Name: _____

at
be
this
have
from

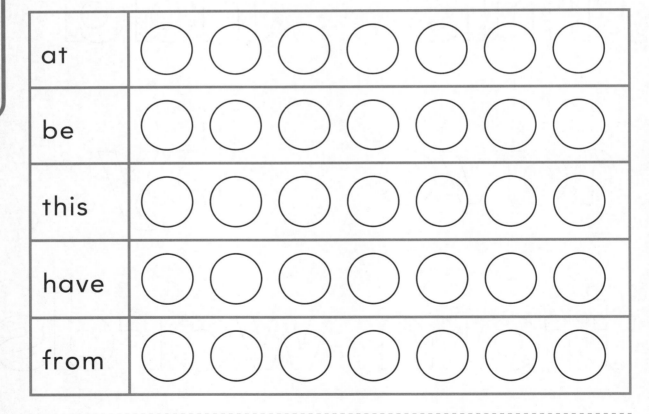

at	◯ ◯ ◯ ◯ ◯ ◯ ◯
be	◯ ◯ ◯ ◯ ◯ ◯ ◯
this	◯ ◯ ◯ ◯ ◯ ◯ ◯
have	◯ ◯ ◯ ◯ ◯ ◯ ◯
from	◯ ◯ ◯ ◯ ◯ ◯ ◯

Directions: Read the words *at, be, this, have*, and *from* with a friend or adult. Find a book or magazine. Search for the words in the text. Color one circle each time you see one of the words. Tell which word you see the most.

Name: _____

Words with an *a*	Words with an *e*	Words with an *i*	Words with an *o*
red	yellow	blue	green

at   this

or   had

be   from

words   we

Directions: Read the words. Use the key to color the words. Make the words with dough.

Name: _____

Materials

- white or light-colored crayon
- watercolors or food coloring mixed in water
- small paintbrush

Directions: Write 5 high-frequency words you know with a white or light-colored crayon. Use watercolors (or food coloring with a small amount of water) to paint over each word. Read the words that pop out.

Name: _____

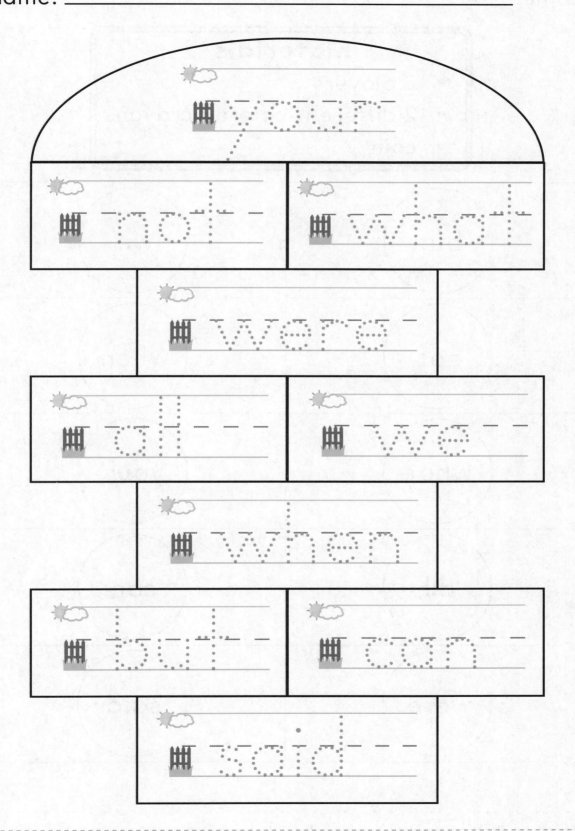

Directions: Trace and read the words. Color the hopscotch game. With an adult or friend, use chalk to create this hopscotch plan and play hopscotch outside.

Name: _____

Materials

- 2 players
- 2 different-colored crayons
- coin

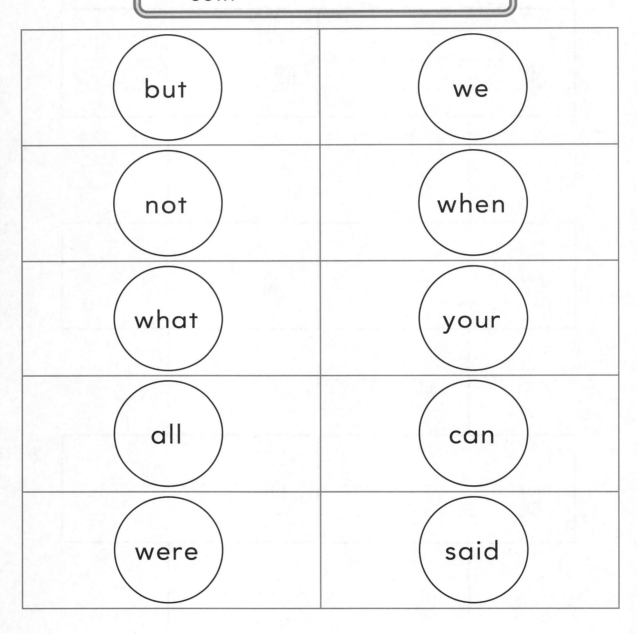

but	we
not	when
what	your
all	can
were	said

Directions: Read the words. Choose a color. Take turns flipping the coin onto the page. If the coin lands on a circle, read the word in the circle and color the circle. Play until all the circles are colored. The player with the most colored circles wins.

Name: _____

but   what   were   when   can
not   all   we   your   said

Directions: Read the words. Find and circle these words hidden in the picture. Color the picture.

Name: _____

Materials

- 2 or more players
- Word Jar with *High-Frequency Word Cards 1–40*

the	of	and	a	to
in	is	you	that	it
he	was	for	on	are
as	with	his	they	I
at	be	this	have	from
or	one	had	by	words
but	not	what	all	were
we	when	your	can	said

Directions: Read the words. Make sure all 40 words are in your Word Jar. Shake some word cards out of your Word Jar onto a table. Read the words that face up. Repeat and take turns with other players.

Name: _____

there	your	can	said
gray	tan	black	pink

Do you see there is a cow on the grass?

Directions: Read the words. Use the key to color the picture. Read the sentence. Circle the word *there* in the sentence.

Name: _____

there

There is a .
dog

Are there ?
30   kids

There is a .
bus

Are there ?
cars   31

Directions: Trace the word *there* with your finger at least 5 times, saying the name of each letter. Read the word. Color the word. Use the word in a sentence. Then, read the pages and circle the word *there* on the pages of the book.

Name: _____

Words 41–50

Practice: use

not

use

use

use

what

all

we

when

use

said

can

use

there

use

Directions: Trace the word *use* with your finger at least 5 times, saying the name of each letter. Read the word. Use the word in a sentence. Find and circle the word *use*.

Name: _____

Words 41–50

Practice: use

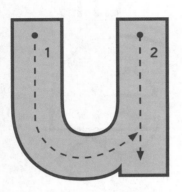  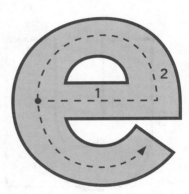

Directions: Trace the word *use* at least 5 times with your finger, saying the name of each letter. Read the word. Use the word in a sentence. Then, trace the words.

Name: _____

there use

May I sit _____?

I will _____ this box.

I want to go _____.

Directions: Trace the words *there* and *use*. Say the name of each letter as you do this. Read each word. Read the sentences. Write *there* or *use* to complete each sentence.

Name: _____

Can you find **an**?

a	n	s	m	t	l
s	j	a	n	c	k
n	a	n	w	d	a
u	s	d	a	n	h
o	a	n	k	a	r
n	t	b	i	a	n

Directions: Read the word *an*. Then, find and circle the word 6 times in the word search.

Words 41–50   Practice: an

Directions: Trace the word *an* with your finger at least 5 times, saying the name of each letter. Read the word. Use the word in a sentence. Cover the word with small objects. Color the word and the pictures. Then, go on a scavenger hunt to find this word in print.

Name: _____

Each 🌿 is ⬤.
plant   green

32

Is each 🌳 📊?
tree   tall

33

Directions: Trace the word *each* with your finger at least 5 times, saying the name of each letter. Read the word. Color the word. Use the word in a sentence. Then, read the pages and circle the word *each* on the pages of the book.

One for  each of you.

Put each in its spot.

Love each other!

Directions: Trace the word *each* in the sentences. Read the sentences. Color the pictures.

Name: _____

Words 41–50

Review: an, each

an

Each

Each

an

An

each

each

An

Directions: Read each word. Draw lines to match the words. Say each word in a sentence.

which

w h i c h e
a w h i c h h
w h i c h b
d w h i c h

Practice: which

Words 41–50

Directions: Read the word *which*. Find and circle the hidden word *which* 4 times. Tell a friend or adult what your favorite high-frequency word is.

Name: _____

1.  _____ do
you like?

2. I see _____
one I like.

3. _____
others should we get?

Time to Draw

_____

Directions: Write the word *which* in each sentence. Read the sentences. Draw something you might like to get.

Name: _____

1. Will  _____ go?

2. _____ is ready to go.

3. I see _____ is having fun.

4. _____ is going again!

Directions: Write the word *she* to finish each sentence. Read the sentences. Color the pictures. Talk to a friend or adult about what you like to do at the park.

Words 41–50

Practice: she

Name: _____

she   which

Directions: Color the spaces with *she* pink. Color the spaces with *which* green. Tell a friend or adult what you see.

130219—180 Days of High-Frequency Words   © Shell Education

Name: _____

1

"Mom, **which** one?"

2

She is our puppy!

3

I wonder **which** we will get.

Animal Shelter

Directions: Read each sentence. Draw lines to put the story in order. Color the pictures.

Name: _____

which	she	an	each	do
blue	**pink**	**yellow**	**green**	**red**

Do you see the train?

Directions: Read the words. Use the key to color the picture. Read the sentence. Circle the word *Do* in the sentence.

Name: _____

do

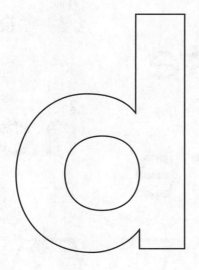

Do you like to ?

read

34

We do like to .

read

35

Directions: Trace the word *do* with your finger at least 5 times, saying the name of each letter. Read the word. Color the word. Use the word in a sentence. Then, read the pages and circle the word *do* on the pages of the book.

Name: _____

Words 41–50

Practice: how

an

how

use

how

there

how

how

how

which

do

how

there

there

use

how

Directions: Trace the word *how* with your finger at least 5 times, saying the name of each letter. Read the word. Use the word in a sentence. Find and circle the word *how*.

Name: _____

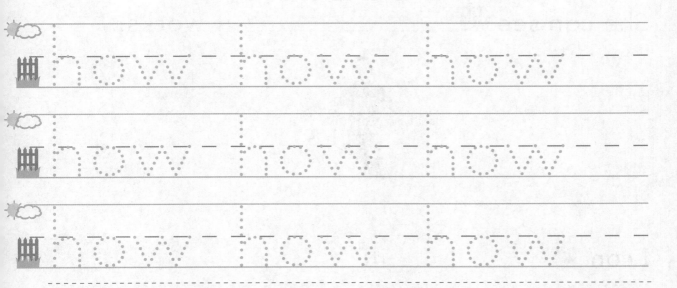

Directions: Trace the word *how* with your finger at least 5 times, saying the name of each letter. Read the word. Use the word in a sentence. Then, trace the words.

Name: _____

Where  I find you?

She can see _____ it works.

I can _____ it!

Directions: Trace the words *do* and *how*. Say the name of each letter as you do this. Read each word. Read the sentences. Write *do* or *how* to complete each sentence.

Name: _____

Can you find **their**?

o	t	h	e	i	r
t	h	e	i	r	j
t	h	e	i	r	f
l	t	h	e	i	r
t	h	e	i	r	g
d	t	h	e	i	r

Directions: Read the word *their*. Then, find and circle the word 6 times in the word search.

Name: _____

their

Directions: Trace the word *their* with your finger at least 5 times, saying the name of each letter. Read the word. Use the word in a sentence. Cover the word with small objects. Color the word and the pictures. Then, go on a scavenger hunt to find this word in print.

130219—180 Days of High-Frequency Words

Name: _____

if it is ❄
cold

36

if it is ☀
warm

37

Directions: Trace the word *if* with your finger at least 5 times, saying the name of each letter. Read the word. Color the word. Use the word in a sentence. Then, read the pages and circle the word *if* on the pages of the book.

Name: _____

 I jump

 I taste it

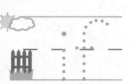 I make it

Directions: Trace the word *if* in the phrases. Read the phrases. Color the pictures.

Name: _____

their   do

if   how

do   if

how   their

Directions: Read each word. Draw lines to match the words. Say each word in a sentence.

130219—180 Days of High-Frequency Words

Words 41–50

Review: their, use, an

Name: _____

their   use   an

Time to Draw

Directions: Read the words. Draw and color your favorite place in nature. Hide the words *there, use*, and *an* inside your picture. Ask a friend or adult to find the hidden words.

Name: _____

| use | an | Each | Which | she |

A Sweet Day

A family went to ☐☐ ice cream shop.

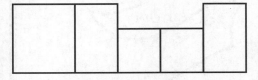 flavor will  get?

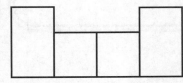 one is delicious.

We will need to ☐☐☐ spoons.

Review: use, an, each, which, she

Words 41–50

Directions: Read the words and the story. Make the missing words by writing one letter in each box. Draw a picture for the story on another sheet of paper. Share it with a friend or adult.

Name: _____

do	how	their	if
pink	yellow	purple	green

Time to Draw

Directions: Read the words. Use the key to color the picture. Draw where this unicorn might live. Share it with a friend or adult.

do   how   their   if

Materials

- 2 or more players
- *High-Frequency Word Memory Game Cards 41–50* (page 191)

Directions: Place the cut-out *High-Frequency Word Memory Game Cards* facedown on the game board. Take turns. Turn over 2 cards at a time to make word matches. Keep the matches you find. Play until you find all the matches.

Name: _____

there	an	which	do	their
use	each	she	how	if

Materials

- 2 players
- 1 number cube
- pencils and crayons (1 color per player)
- *High-Frequency Word Cards 41–50* (page 215)

Words 41–50

Review

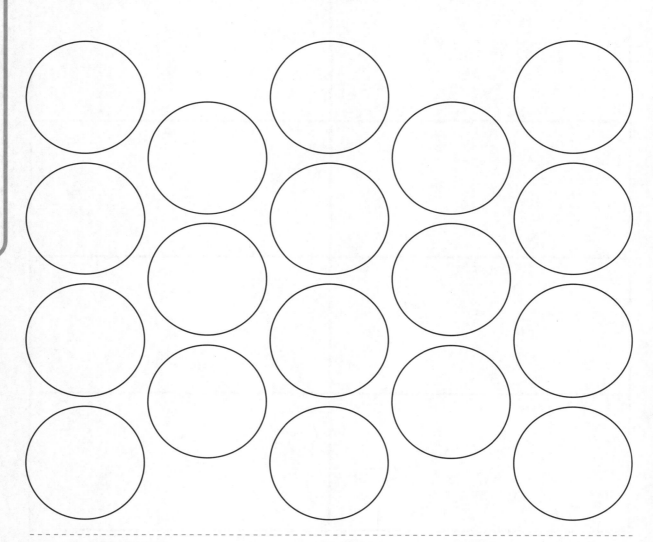

Directions: Put the cut-out *High-Frequency Word Cards* facedown in a pile. The first player rolls the number cube and chooses a card. Then, they write the word in a circle and color the number of circles on the cube. Players take turns until all circles are colored. The player with the most colored circles wins.

High-Frequency Word Memory Game Cards 41–50

do do

how how

their their

if if

High-Frequency Word
Memory Game Cards
41–50

High-Frequency Word
Memory Game Cards
41–50

High-Frequency Word
Memory Game Cards
41–50

High-Frequency Word
Memory Game Cards
41–50

High-Frequency Word
Memory Game Cards
41–50

High-Frequency Word
Memory Game Cards
41–50

High-Frequency Word
Memory Game Cards
41–50

High-Frequency Word
Memory Game Cards
41–50

Name: _____

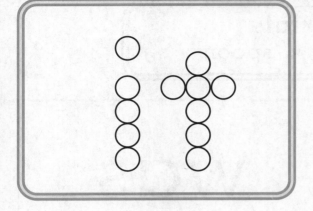

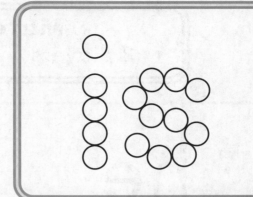

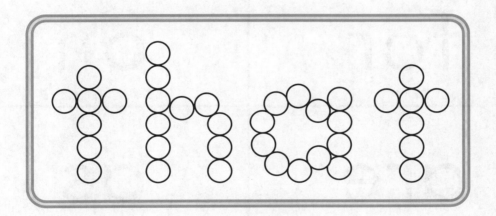

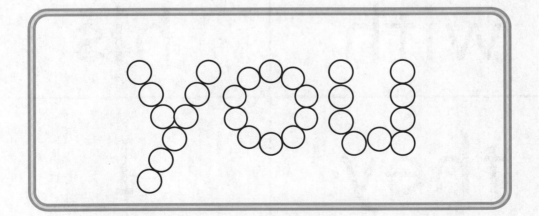

Directions: Read the words *it*, *is*, *that*, and *you*. Color or paint all the circles to make the letters for each word. Use the words in sentences. Share the sentences with a friend or adult.

I Know 50 Words!

Name: _____

Materials
- 2 players
- spoon

he	was
for	on
are	as
with	his
they	I

Directions: Read the words with a friend or adult. One player reads the words in any order, while the other player taps the words with a spoon. See how many words you can read and tap in 1 minute.

Name: _____

at

or

be

one

this

had

have

by

from

words

Directions: Read the words with an adult. In a dark room, use a flashlight to trace the letters with light. Then, color the words.

Name: _____

but
not
what
all
were

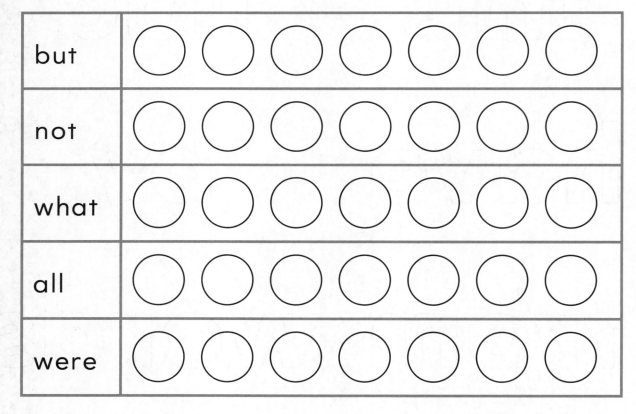

but	◯ ◯ ◯ ◯ ◯ ◯ ◯
not	◯ ◯ ◯ ◯ ◯ ◯ ◯
what	◯ ◯ ◯ ◯ ◯ ◯ ◯
all	◯ ◯ ◯ ◯ ◯ ◯ ◯
were	◯ ◯ ◯ ◯ ◯ ◯ ◯

Directions: Read the words *but, not, what, all*, and *were* with a friend or adult. Find a book or magazine. Search for the words in the text. Color one circle each time you see one of the words. Tell which word you see the most.

Name: _____

Words with an *a*	Words with an *e*	Words with an *i*	Words with an *o*
red	yellow	blue	green

we   there

which   do

when   how

she   an

can   if

Directions: Read the words. Use the key to color the words. Make the words with dough.

Name: _____

Materials

- white or light-colored crayon
- watercolors or food coloring mixed in water
- small paintbrush

Directions: Write 5 high-frequency words you know with a white or light-colored crayon. Use watercolors (or food coloring with a small amount of water) to paint over each word. Read the words that pop out.

Name: _____

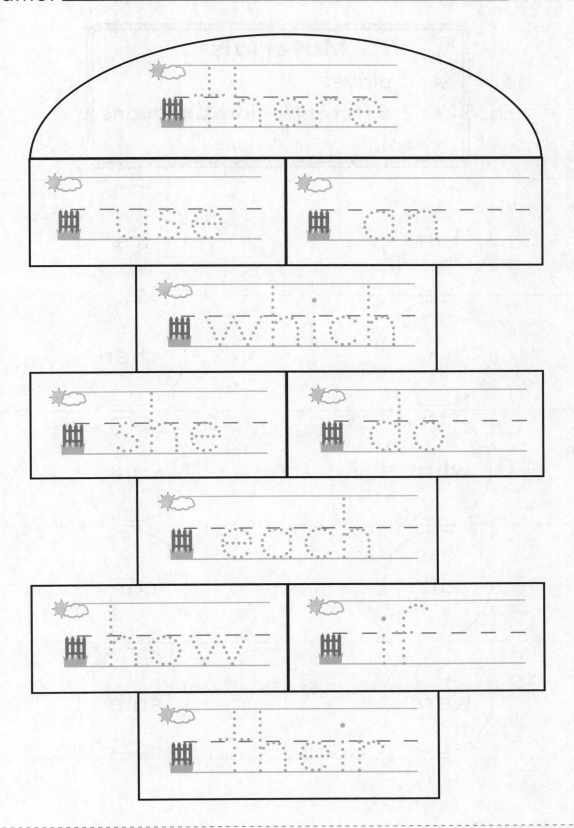

Directions: Trace and read the words. Color the hopscotch game. With an adult or friend, use chalk to create this hopscotch plan and play hopscotch outside.

Cumulative Review of Words 1–50

I Know 50 Words!

Name: ____________________

Materials

- 2 players
- 2 different-colored crayons
- coin

but	we
not	when
what	your
all	can
were	said

Directions: Read the words. Choose a color. Take turns flipping the coin onto the page. If the coin lands on a circle, read the word in the circle and color the circle. Play until all the circles are colored. The player with the most colored circles wins.

Name: _____

at	from	by	have	had
this	one	be	or	words

Directions: Read the words. Find and circle these words hidden in the picture. Color the picture.

Name: _____

Materials

- 2 or more players
- Word Jar with all High-Frequency Word Cards

I Know 50 Words!

the	of	and	a	to
in	is	you	that	it
he	was	for	on	are
as	with	his	they	I
at	be	this	have	from
or	one	had	by	words
but	not	what	all	were
we	when	your	can	said
there	use	an	each	which
she	do	how	their	if

Directions: Read the words. Make sure all 50 words are in your Word Jar. Shake some word cards out of your Word Jar onto a table. Read the words that are faceup. Repeat and take turns with other players.

Congratulations!

You did it!

Congratulations to:

_____

Achievement:

You worked hard for 180 days to learn high-frequency words!

Way to go! You did your best!

Awarded by: _____   **Date:** _____

- -

Directions: Read each word aloud with an adult. Draw yourself as a reader. Post this certificate somewhere special.

Student Recording Sheet

Directions: The following word list can be used to assess students and record their progress. Have students use the *High-Frequency Word Cards* on pages 207–216 while you use this list to mark which words have been mastered.

Name: _____

Date:	Date:	Date:	Date:	Date:
Words 1–10 _____/10	**Words 11–20** _____/10	**Words 21–30** _____/10	**Words 31–40** _____/10	**Words 41–50** _____/10
_____ the	_____ he	_____ at	_____ but	_____ there
_____ of	_____ was	_____ be	_____ not	_____ use
_____ and	_____ for	_____ this	_____ what	_____ an
_____ a	_____ on	_____ have	_____ all	_____ each
_____ to	_____ are	_____ from	_____ were	_____ which
_____ in	_____ as	_____ or	_____ we	_____ she
_____ is	_____ with	_____ one	_____ when	_____ do
_____ you	_____ his	_____ had	_____ your	_____ how
_____ that	_____ they	_____ by	_____ can	_____ their
_____ it	_____ I	_____ words	_____ said	_____ if

Class Recording Sheet

Directions: Record students' progress on the chart. Use the last column to record words that have not yet been mastered.

Student Name	Date: _____	Date: _____	Date: _____	Date: _____	Focus Words

High-Frequency Word Bingo

Materials

- 2 or more players
- High-Frequency Word Cards

Directions: Choose any of the high-frequency words from this book. Write the words in a random order on this gameboard. (Additional copies can be printed from the Digital Resources.) Play Bingo by drawing word cards until the student(s) have 3 words in a row.

High-Frequency Word Cards 1–10

the	in
of	is
and	you
a	that
to	it

High-Frequency Word
Cards 1–10

High-Frequency Word
Cards 1–10

High-Frequency Word
Cards 1–10

High-Frequency Word
Cards 1–10

High-Frequency Word
Cards 1–10

High-Frequency Word
Cards 1–10

High-Frequency Word
Cards 1–10

High-Frequency Word
Cards 1–10

High-Frequency Word
Cards 1–10

High-Frequency Word
Cards 1–10

he	as
was	with
for	his
on	they
are	I

High-Frequency Word
Cards 11–20

High-Frequency Word
Cards 11–20

High-Frequency Word
Cards 11–20

High-Frequency Word
Cards 11–20

High-Frequency Word
Cards 11–20

High-Frequency Word
Cards 11–20

High-Frequency Word
Cards 11–20

High-Frequency Word
Cards 11–20

High-Frequency Word
Cards 11–20

High-Frequency Word
Cards 11–20

High-Frequency Word Cards 21–30

at	or
be	one
this	had
have	by
from	words

High-Frequency Word
Cards 21–30

High-Frequency Word
Cards 21–30

High-Frequency Word
Cards 21–30

High-Frequency Word
Cards 21–30

High-Frequency Word
Cards 21–30

High-Frequency Word
Cards 21–30

High-Frequency Word
Cards 21–30

High-Frequency Word
Cards 21–30

High-Frequency Word
Cards 21–30

High-Frequency Word
Cards 21–30

High-Frequency Word Cards 31–40

but	we
not	when
what	your
all	can
were	said

High-Frequency Word
Cards 31–40

High-Frequency Word
Cards 31–40

High-Frequency Word
Cards 31–40

High-Frequency Word
Cards 31–40

High-Frequency Word
Cards 31–40

High-Frequency Word
Cards 31–40

High-Frequency Word
Cards 31–40

High-Frequency Word
Cards 31–40

High-Frequency Word
Cards 31–40

High-Frequency Word
Cards 31–40

there	she
use	do
an	how
each	their
which	if

High-Frequency Word
Cards 41–50

High-Frequency Word
Cards 41–50

High-Frequency Word
Cards 41–50

High-Frequency Word
Cards 41–50

High-Frequency Word
Cards 41–50

High-Frequency Word
Cards 41–50

High-Frequency Word
Cards 41–50

High-Frequency Word
Cards 41–50

High-Frequency Word
Cards 41–50

High-Frequency Word
Cards 41–50

References Cited

First Things First. 2017. "Early Childhood Brain Development Has Lifelong Impact." *Arizona PBS*. azpbs.org/2017/11/early-childhood-brain-development-lifelong-impact.

Fry, Edward. 1999. *1,000 Instant Words: The Most Common Words for Teaching Reading, Writing, and Spelling*. Garden Grove, CA: Teacher Created Resources.

Fry, Edward B., and Jacqueline W. Kress. 2006. *The Reading Teacher's Book of Lists*, 5th edition. San Francisco: Jossey-Bass.

Hirsch, Megan. 2010. *How to Hold a Pencil*. Los Angeles, CA: Hirsch Indie Press.

Warley, Heather P., Marcia A. Invernizzi, and E. Allison Drake. 2015. "Sight Word Learning: There's More to it than Meets the Eye." *Reading in Virginia* 37: 40–45.

Answer Key

page 13

Students should circle *the*.

page 14
Students should circle *the*.

page 15

page 17
at *the* beach
lots *of* cats
over *the* moon

page 18

page 20
Students should circle *a*.

page 23

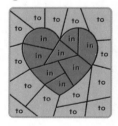

q t o e t k
a o m n t o
t o c h l g
p b t o w x

page 25
a puppy *in* a bed
children *in* the pool
a goldfish *in* a fishbowl
a bird *in* a nest

page 26

page 27
He went to the store.
He put the gumball in his mouth.
He made a big bubble.

page 28

Students should circle *is*.

page 29
Students should circle *is*.

page 30

page 32
This *is* me!
I see *you*.
She *is* running.

page 33

t	h	a	t	e	g
f	o	t	h	a	t
l	t	h	a	t	u
p	w	t	h	a	t
t	h	a	t	x	l
s	t	h	a	t	j

page 35
Students should circle *it*.

page 39

A Day of Movie Fun

I went to see a movie.

I got snacks and a drink.

I went in the theater.

page 40

Answer Key *(cont.)*

page 45

q b (h e) f k
(h e) m n g a
r u d i (h e)
s (h e) v j y

page 48

page 49

He went to swim.
He put on floaties.
Then, he got to swim.

page 50

Students should circle the word
for.

page 51

Students should circle the word
for.

page 52

page 54

Look *for* a toy.
Sit *on* that.
It is lunch *for* two.

page 55

page 57

Students should circle the word
as.

page 60

page 63

page 64

He went with his mom.
He put them in his cart.
Then, he pushed the cart.

page 65

Students should circle the word
they.

page 66

Students should circle the word
they.

page 67

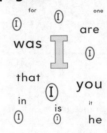

page 69

Are *they* ready?
They are happy.
I am ready.

page 71

The Farm

A boy is [on] the farm.

Pigs are in the mud, [as]
dirty [as] can be.

[He] looks [for] horses.

Where [are] the cows?

page 72

© Shell Education

130219—180 Days of High-Frequency Words

Answer Key *(cont.)*

page 81

you   the
and   of
it   to
a   that
in   is

page 85

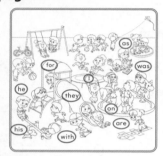

page 87

w	a	t	g	u	c
a	t	f	s	m	r
u	c	d	k	a	t
a	t	o	b	n	d
y	p	a	t	w	h
z	f	k	a	t	q

page 89

Students should circle the word *be.*

page 92

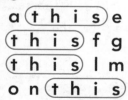

a t h i s e
t h i s f g
t h i s l m
o n t h i s

page 95

page 96

The friends went to this game.
They cheered.
"We have won this!" they said.

page 97

Students should circle the word *from.*

page 98

Students should circle the word *from.*

page 99

page 101

He came *from* the bus.
Do you like dogs *or* cats?
I see a note *from* my grandpa.

page 102

l	e	p	o	n	e
f	s	j	o	n	e
c	f	o	n	e	d
o	n	e	d	u	t
r	o	n	e	k	a
s	m	o	n	e	r

page 104

Students should circle the word *had.*

page 107

b y a c b e
l m b y s d
t h o n b y
j k h b y s

page 110

page 111

I went by the park.
I saw a friend by the tables.
We read the words on the sign.

page 113

At the Lake

A girl was at the lake.

She knew from the
sunshine this was going
to be a nice day.

Do I have my big hat, or
do I need an umbrella?

Answer Key *(cont.)*

page 114

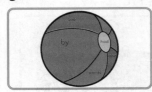

page 119

Students should circle the word *but*.

page 120

Students should circle the word *but*.

page 121

page 123

Do you like it or *not*?
She had it, *but* there was no rain.
I am *not* the baby now.

page 124

o	w	h	a	t	d
k	n	w	h	a	t
w	h	a	t	j	s
y	i	w	h	a	t
c	w	h	a	t	u
w	h	a	t	j	f

page 126

Students should circle the word *all*.

page 129

page 130

Students should circle the word *were*.

page 131

page 133

They *were* fast.
Do *we* hear it?
Yes, *we* went to a movie.

page 134

w	h	e	n	v	g
f	r	w	h	e	n
c	w	h	e	n	d
u	l	w	h	e	n
w	h	e	n	k	b
s	w	h	e	n	r

page 136

Students should circle the word *your*.

page 139

page 142

page 143

"I can do this," she said.
"I can do this, too," he said.
"We can both do this," they said.

page 145

Camping

We set up our camp.
All of us were happy.
It was cold, but we kept warm.
What a campfire we made!

We love camping and do not want to go home.

page 146

Answer Key *(cont.)*

page 155

at   this

or   had

be   from

words   we

page 159

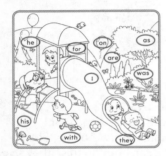

page 161

Students should circle the word *there.*

page 162

Students should circle the word *there.*

page 163

page 165

May I sit *there*?
I will *use* this box.
I want to go *there*.

page 166

page 168

Students should circle the word *each.*

page 171

w h i c h e
a w h i c h
w h i c h b
d w h i c h

page 174

page 175

I wonder which we will get.
"Mom, which one?"
She is our puppy!

page 176

Students should circle the word *do.*

page 177

Students should circle the word *do.*

page 178

page 180

Where *do* I find you?
She can see *how* it works.
I can *do* it!

page 181

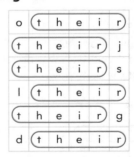

page 183

Students should circle the word *if.*

Answer Key *(cont.)*

page 187

A Sweet Day

A family went to [a][n] ice cream shop.

[W][h][i][c][h] flavor will [s][h][e] get?

[E][a][c][h] one is delicious.

We will need to [u][s][e] spoons.

page 188

page 197

we	do
which	there
when	how
she	an
can	if

page 201

Digital Resources

Accessing the Digital Resources

The digital resources can be downloaded by following these steps:

1. Go to **www.tcmpub.com/digital**

2. Use the ISBN number to redeem the digital resources.

3. Respond to the question using the book.

4. Follow the prompts on the Content Cloud website to sign in or create a new account.

5. The content redeemed will now be on your My Content screen. Click on the product to look through the digital resources. All resources are available for download. Select files can be previewed, opened, and shared.

For questions and assistance with your license key card, or to report a lost card, please contact Shell Education.

> **email:** customerservice@tcmpub.com
>
> **phone:** 800-858-7339

Contents of the Digital Resources

Activities

- Bingo gameboard
- Ideas for extending the learning to real-world situations
- Templates for creating high-frequency word books
- Hands-on practice for learning uppercase and lowercase letters
- Writing practice of uppercase and lowercase letters

Teacher Resources

- Certificate of Completion
- Student and Class Recording Sheets
- Rubric
- High-Frequency Word Cards
- Standards Correlations